The Hilarious Art of War!

Sun Tzu the Art of War remastered in a modern way

by

Morgan Adams

Copyright © 2023 by Morgan Adams

All rights reserved. No part of this publication may be reproduced, distributed, or transmitted in any form or by any means, including photocopying, recording, or other electronic or mechanical methods, without the prior written permission of the publisher, except in the case of brief quotations embodied in critical reviews and certain other noncommercial uses permitted by copyright law.

Introduction

Welcome to "The Hilarious Art of War"! If you're here, it means you're interested in Sun Tzu's timeless strategies for warfare, but you're not exactly thrilled about reading a dry, ancient text. Fear not, dear reader, because this book is here to make learning about the Art of War a hilarious and engaging experience.

So, why did I write this book? Well, as someone who has studied Sun Tzu's work, I've always found it fascinating how applicable his insights are to not just warfare, but also everyday life. However, I've also noticed that many people find his writing dense and intimidating, which is a shame because there's so much to learn from it. That's why I decided to put a modern, funny spin on his teachings - to make them more accessible and entertaining for everyone.

Throughout this book, I'll be analyzing Sun Tzu's strategies in a way that's both informative and lighthearted. You'll learn about everything from the importance of knowing yourself and your enemy, to the art of deception and the dangers of overconfidence. And along the way, I'll be cracking jokes, making pop culture references, and using relatable examples to help you understand these concepts in a whole new way.

By the end of this book, you'll not only have a deeper appreciation for Sun Tzu's genius, but you'll also have some practical tips for applying his strategies to your own life. So, buckle up, grab a snack, and get ready to laugh and learn your way through "The Hilarious Art of War"!

I. Laying Plans

1. Yo, listen up, the art of war is hella important for the State, according to Sun Tzu.

2. It's like, do or die, either you're chillin' or you're screwed. So, you better not slack on studying this stuff.

3. Basically, there are five things you need to keep in mind when deciding how to conquer the battlefield.

4. These five things are:

 (1) The Moral Law;

(2) Heaven;

(3) Earth;

(4) The Commander;

(5) Method and discipline.

5,6. The Moral Law is all about getting your people to back you up no matter what, even if it means risking their lives.

7. Heaven is all about the weather and the seasons, like whether it's hot or cold, or if it's night or day.

8. Earth is about everything else, like how far away things are, if you're in danger, if you're in a tight spot, and if there's any chance you could die.

Explanation:

Sun Tzu was one smart cookie when it came to warfare. He's basically saying that if you wanna be a boss and dominate the battlefield, you gotta study this art of war business.

It's not just a game, it's do or die, like your life depends on it. So, don't sleep on this stuff and make sure you know it inside out.

Basically, there's five things you gotta keep in mind if you wanna come out on top:

(1) Get your peeps to have your back, even if it means risking it all.

(2) Keep an eye on the weather and the seasons, cuz that can make or break your plan.

(3) Be aware of everything else, like your surroundings and how much danger you're in.

But wait, there's more! The last two things you need to think about are:

(4) having a boss commander who knows their stuff and

(5) having a solid plan of attack and sticking to it like glue.

So, if you wanna be a general badass and rule the battlefield, study up on the art of war and remember these five things.

9. The Commander should embody the virtues of a wise, sincere, benevolent, courageous, and strict leader. Think of yourself as a boss with a great personality and a stern hand.

This means that as a leader, you should be smart, honest, kind, brave, and firm. For example, a good boss is someone who listens to their employees' concerns, gives constructive feedback, and sets clear expectations. At the same time, they need to make tough decisions when necessary and hold their team accountable for their actions. Think of Steve Jobs, the co-founder of Apple, who was known for his visionary leadership style and high standards.

10. Method and discipline are crucial to your success. This means you should organize your squad properly, assign ranks and roles, make sure you have enough snacks and drinks, and keep an eye on your budget. Remember, war can be expensive!

In other words, to be successful, you need to have a plan, follow through with it, and maintain order and structure. For example, if you're running a small business, you need to set clear goals, assign tasks to your team, and track your expenses. If you don't have a system in place, chaos can ensue, and you might end up losing money or customers.

11. These five principles are critical for every leader. If you know them, you'll win. If you don't, you'll lose. It's as simple as that.

These five principles are the cornerstone of effective leadership, and if you master them, you'll be ahead of the game. They are like the cheat codes to winning in the business world. For example, if you're running a startup, you need to focus on building a strong team, providing a great product or service, creating a solid brand, staying ahead of the competition, and managing your finances. If you neglect any of these areas, your chances of success are slim.

12. So, when planning your next attack, compare these five factors:

(1) which ruler is more morally upright,

(2) which general is more skilled,

(3) who has the best location,

(4) who has the most disciplined troops, and

(5) who has more soldiers or weapons. It's like comparing stats in a video game!

When you're competing against others, it's important to evaluate your strengths and weaknesses compared to your opponents. For example, if you're applying for a job, you need to consider your skills, experience, and personality traits, as well as those of the other candidates. If you know that the other candidates have more experience, but you have a better attitude and work ethic, you can use that to your advantage.

13. Based on these seven considerations, you can predict your victory or defeat. It's like predicting your chances of winning the lottery, only with more violence.

14. Listen to my advice and act upon it, and you'll be a winner. Keep me as your advisor! Ignore my advice, and you'll be a loser. Fire me immediately!

By analyzing the factors that can affect your success, you can make an informed decision and increase your chances of winning. For example, if you're thinking of starting a new business, you need to consider the market demand, your budget, your competition, your team, your location, and your marketing strategy. If you have a good understanding of these factors, you can make a more accurate prediction of your success.

Remember, the key to success is being both cool and collected, so keep your wits about you and lead your army with confidence!

15. Listen to my advice, but also be on the lookout for any unexpected opportunities to make bank.

This means that while it's important to follow the advice of experienced leaders, it's also important to keep an eye out for opportunities to profit or gain an advantage. For example, if you're a business owner, you may follow the advice of a successful entrepreneur, but you also need to be creative and adaptable in order to stay ahead of your competitors.

16. If things are going your way, go with the flow and adjust your plans accordingly.

Sometimes you need to be flexible and adjust your plans based on the situation. For example, if you're planning a party and it starts raining, you might need to move the festivities indoors.

17. Let's be real, war is just one big game of pretending.

Sometimes in war, you need to pretend to be weaker or stronger than you actually are in order to deceive your enemy. For example, you might create a fake army to distract your enemy while your real army attacks from a different direction.

18. When you're ready to attack, act like you're not. When you're fighting, act like you're not. When you're close, act like you're far. When you're far, act like you're close. Confuse the heck out of your enemy!

You need to keep your enemy guessing and confused about your intentions. For example, if you're negotiating a business deal, you might act disinterested in order to make the other party more eager to make a deal.

19. Trick your enemy into making mistakes by making yourself look weak or disorganized.

You can use deception to make your enemy underestimate you and make mistakes. For example, you might intentionally leave a few items out of stock on your online store to create a sense of urgency and encourage customers to make a purchase.

20. If your opponent is stronger, run away. If your opponent is weak, take advantage of that.

You need to assess your enemy's strengths and weaknesses and adjust your strategy accordingly. For example, if you're playing a video game and your opponent has stronger weapons, you might retreat and try to find better equipment before engaging in battle.

21. If your enemy is easily angered, push their buttons. Act like you're weaker than them to boost their ego.

This means that you can use psychological tactics to get under your enemy's skin and make them more prone to making mistakes. For example, you might compliment your opponent's skills to boost their ego and then take advantage of their overconfidence.

22. Don't give your opponent a break, keep pushing and don't let them relax. If their forces are together, find a way to split them up.

This means that you need to keep the pressure on your enemy and not let them regroup or recover. For example, in a sports game, you might keep attacking the same weak spot on the opponent's defense to keep them off balance.

23. Catch your enemy off guard by attacking where they least expect it.

You can use surprise attacks to catch your enemy off guard and gain an advantage. For example, if you're playing a game of chess, you might set up a trap for your opponent by sacrificing a piece and then launching a surprise attack.

24. Keep your tricks up your sleeve and don't reveal your plans too soon.

You need to be strategic and keep your plans secret until the right moment. For example, in a business negotiation, you might keep your best offer hidden until the last minute to avoid giving the other party an advantage.

25. The general who wins thinks ahead and plans meticulously, while the general who loses doesn't prepare enough. Remember, it's all about the calculations!

II. Waging War

1. If you want to go to war with a thousand swift chariots, as many heavy chariots, and a hundred thousand soldiers in mail, and you want to feed them for a thousand li, you'll need a grand total of a thousand ounces of silver per day. Oh, and don't forget the glue and paint for those chariots!

Money makes the world go round, even in war. If you want to maintain a large army, you better have deep pockets. And don't forget about the small things like glue and paint for your chariots! In modern times, this could be compared to the importance of having a well-funded military with the necessary equipment and supplies.

2. Listen, if a fight drags on too long, your weapons will get dull, and your troops will start losing their mojo. And if you're trying to siege a town, you're gonna wear yourself out.

Don't drag out a fight for too long. You don't want to wear out your troops or your weapons. It's like playing a game of tug-of-war for too long and getting too tired to keep going. In modern times, this could be compared to the importance of having a clear plan and timeline for a military operation.

3. And if the war just keeps dragging on and on, your country's resources are gonna dry up like the Sahara.

Prolonged wars are costly. Wars drain resources, and if they go on for too long, a country's economy can suffer greatly. It's like spending all your money on a single shopping spree and then realizing you have nothing left for the rest of the month. In modern times, this could be compared to the importance of considering the long-term effects of a military conflict on a country's economy and resources.

4. Once you're out of weapons, energy, and money, you're gonna be in a world of hurt. And that's when all the other chieftains start smelling blood in the water.

Wars should be strategic, not impulsive. Rushing into a fight without a plan is just plain stupid. In modern times, this could be compared to the importance of having a clear objective and strategy before engaging in military conflict.

5. Look, rushing into a fight is dumb, but dragging it out for too long isn't clever either.

6. Seriously, no one has ever won from a prolonged war. It's like trying to win a marathon by taking a nap halfway through.

7. Only someone who's been through war and understands its horrors can figure out how to actually profit from it. And let's be real, it's not really a profit if it costs lives and destruction.

Winning a war should not come at the cost of human lives and destruction. The idea of profiting from a war may seem appealing, but in reality, the cost is too high. In modern times, this could be compared to the importance of considering the ethical implications of military action and prioritizing the preservation of human life and minimizing collateral damage.

8. The smart soldier doesn't call for backup or load up on snacks more than twice. Anything more than that and they're just a liability.

This means that a soldier should only call for backup or take breaks to eat snacks a limited number of times, otherwise they'll become a burden on the rest of the team. In modern times, this could be compared to taking too many breaks at work or relying on others to do your work for you. It's important to be self-sufficient and not overburden your team.

9. Bring your own snacks to the war, but steal the enemy's pizza. This way, your army won't go hungry and you'll have extra toppings for victory celebrations.

You should bring your own snacks to avoid going hungry, but also to steal the enemy's pizza as an extra victory celebration. This could be applied to everyday life by being prepared and resourceful, but also taking advantage of unexpected opportunities.

10. If the government is broke, they'll beg for money to keep the army going. But if the army is too far away, they'll have to start selling Girl Scout cookies to afford their weapons.

    This saying is a play on the idea that governments need money to fund their armies. If the government is broke, they may have to resort to unconventional means of fundraising. In modern times, this could be compared to companies cutting corners or looking for alternative sources of funding when they're struggling financially. It's like watching your dad dress up as a clown for a kid's birthday party just to make ends meet.

11. When the army's too close, prices go up like a rocket ship, and the people's wallets go down like a sinking ship. It's like living next to a Whole Foods during a zombie apocalypse.

    When the army is too close to a town, prices go up and people's wallets go down, which is similar to the situation of living next to an expensive grocery store during a disaster. It's important to be aware of how external factors can affect your financial situation and to be prepared for unexpected expenses. It's like trying to buy a bottle of water at a music festival - you know you're getting ripped off, but you gotta stay hydrated.

12. The peasants will suffer like they just sat on a Lego if the army keeps taking their stuff. Their bank accounts will look like a Black Friday sale at Walmart.

This saying emphasizes the idea that the common people are the ones who suffer the most during times of war. If the army takes their resources and belongings, they'll be left with very little, which is similar to the chaos of a Black Friday sale. It's important to consider the impact of your actions on others and try to minimize harm as much as possible.

13, 14. When the army drains the people's resources and takes all their stuff, the people will have to start wearing fig leaves and eating tree bark. Meanwhile, the government will be blowing all their money on new tanks and shiny helmets.

When the army drains the people's resources, the people will be left with nothing and may have to resort to extreme measures just to survive. Meanwhile, the government may continue to invest in expensive military equipment. This highlights the idea of a power imbalance between the government and the people, and the importance of considering the consequences of government actions on the population. It's like watching your boss blow the company's profits on a new sports car while you're stuck working overtime just to make rent.

15. A wise general knows how to mooch off the enemy. One cartload of their food is worth 20 of our own. It's like winning the lottery, but instead of cash, you get a bunch of Slim Jims.

This means that it's smarter to take the enemy's resources instead of using your own. By taking the enemy's food, you save your own resources for later. It's like getting free snacks from your neighbor instead of buying your own. It's a win-win situation, except for the enemy.

16. If you want your soldiers to kick butt, you gotta get them fired up. And if you want them to stick around, you gotta bribe them with pizza and beer.

 Sun Tzu is saying that in order to defeat the enemy, soldiers must be motivated and incentivized. They need to have a reason to fight and win, whether it's for honor, pride, or rewards. It's like when your boss tells you that if you work hard and meet your targets, you'll get a bonus at the end of the year. It gives you something to work towards and motivates you to do your best.

17. In a chariot race, whoever wins gets a participation trophy and a free slice of pizza. And if we capture the enemy's chariots, we'll give them a makeover and turn them into sweet ride-sharing vehicles. This is called winning at life by using your enemies' resources. It's like taking your ex's Netflix password and using it forever.

 This passage is about how to handle the aftermath of a battle. Sun Tzu suggests that if you capture enemy chariots and soldiers, you should reward the soldiers who were involved in the capture. You should also replace the enemy flags with your own and use the captured chariots as part of your own army. And most importantly, you should treat the captured soldiers with kindness and respect, because they could potentially become valuable assets to your own army.

In modern terms, this is like when a company acquires another company. The acquiring company will often reward the employees who were involved in the acquisition and try to integrate the acquired company's products or services into their own offerings. They'll also try to treat the acquired employees with respect and make them feel valued so that they'll be more likely to stay with the company and contribute to its success.

18. The goal of war is not to take forever, like waiting for your crush to text you back. It's to win quickly and get back to playing video games.

War should be quick and decisive. If it drags on for too long, it becomes a waste of time and resources. It's like waiting for a text from your crush for days, instead of moving on and enjoying your own life. Winning quickly means you can move on to more important things, like playing video games.

19. The leader of the army is like the captain of the Titanic. If they steer the ship wrong, everyone's gonna be swimming with the fishes.

The leader of the army is responsible for the success or failure of the mission. If they make the wrong decisions, everyone suffers. It's like the captain of the Titanic who made the wrong call and caused the ship to sink. The leader must be careful and make smart choices to ensure the safety and success of their troops.

Sun Tzu's III. Attack by Stratagem:

1. Sun Tzu said: In the practical art of war, the best thing of all is to take the enemy's country and its Wi-Fi password whole and intact; to shatter and destroy it is not so good. So, too, it is better to recapture an army's Snapchat account entire than to destroy it, to capture a regiment's Instagram followers, a detachment's Twitter handle, or a company's TikTok videos entire than to destroy them.

    Sun Tzu believes that it is best to take the enemy's country and army intact, rather than destroying it. This is because taking it over allows you to use their resources and manpower for your own benefit. Similarly, it is better to capture an enemy army whole, rather than killing all its soldiers, as the captured soldiers can be integrated into your own forces. In modern times, this could be seen as acquiring a company or organization instead of destroying it, allowing you to use their resources and manpower to benefit your own goals.

2. Hence to fight and conquer in all your battles is not supreme excellence; supreme excellence consists in breaking the enemy's resistance without fighting. Or, you know, just buy their company and take over their market share.

    Sun Tzu suggests that true excellence in warfare lies not in fighting and conquering in every battle, but in breaking the enemy's resistance without fighting at all. This can be achieved through tactics such as diplomacy, espionage, and deception. In modern times, this could be seen as winning a business or political negotiation without resorting to aggression or force.

3. Thus the highest form of generalship is to balk the enemy's plans; the next best is to prevent the junction of the enemy's forces; the next in order is to attack the enemy's army in the field; and the worst policy of all is to have a meeting to discuss how to attack a walled city.

Sun Tzu outlines the hierarchy of successful generalship, stating that the highest form is to thwart the enemy's plans, followed by preventing the enemy's forces from joining together, attacking the enemy in the field, and the worst policy being to besiege a walled city. This is because a siege is often costly and ineffective, leading to many casualties and prolonged fighting. In modern times, this could be seen as avoiding direct conflict with a competitor, instead focusing on outmaneuvering and outsmarting them.

4. The rule is, not to besiege walled cities if it can possibly be avoided. Seriously, just find a backdoor into their network and hack your way in.

Sun Tzu advises against besieging walled cities unless absolutely necessary, as it requires a significant amount of time and resources. Instead, a general should look for alternative strategies to defeat their enemy. In the modern world, this could mean finding alternative solutions to a problem that don't require a lot of resources or time, rather than wasting resources on something that may not be effective. Sun Tzu is basically saying "Don't waste your time and resources on attacking a fortified enemy head-on, instead, use your brain and find a backdoor to their network to hack your way in."

5. The general, unable to control his irritation, will launch his men to the assault like swarming ants, with the result that one-third of his men are slain, while the town still remains untaken. Such are the disastrous effects of a siege. And let's not forget the mental anguish of not having access to proper plumbing or the internet for months on end.

    In the modern world, this principle can apply to many areas of life, such as in business or personal relationships. Reacting impulsively to a problem without considering the potential consequences can be detrimental and may not lead to a successful outcome. It's important to take a step back, evaluate the situation, and approach it with a clear and calculated strategy.

    Sun Tzu also alludes to the mental toll that a long siege can take on an army, highlighting the importance of psychological warfare in military strategy. This is still relevant today, where a sustained campaign of misinformation and psychological manipulation can be just as damaging as physical warfare. In the end, the key takeaway is to remain level-headed and thoughtful in one's approach to conflict, whether it be in war or in everyday life.

6. Therefore the skillful leader subdues the enemy's troops without any fighting; he captures their cities without laying siege to them; he overthrows their kingdom by launching a viral social media campaign.

7. With his forces intact he will dispute the mastery of the Empire, and thus, without losing a man, his triumph will be complete. This is the method of attacking by stratagem. Who needs swords and shields when you have memes and cat videos?

Sun Tzu is advising that a skilled leader can subdue their enemy without resorting to actual fighting. In modern times, this could mean using social media to launch a viral campaign to change public opinion or sway the views of the enemy. With this approach, the leader can capture their cities without resorting to actual siege warfare, and overthrow the enemy's kingdom without any physical violence.

8. It is the rule in war, if our forces are ten to the enemy's one, to surround him; if five to one, to attack him; if twice as numerous, to divide our army into two. And if you're outnumbered, just hide behind a bush until the enemy passes by.

If you're in a war and your forces outnumber your enemy's, Sun Tzu says you should surround them, like when you and your friends circle around that one person in a dodgeball game. If your forces are only slightly greater, you should just go ahead and attack them, like when your squad takes on that one annoying person in Fortnite. And if you're double their size, you should split your forces into two teams, like when you play a game of basketball with more people than usual.

9. If equally matched, we can offer battle; if slightly inferior in numbers, we can avoid the enemy; if quite unequal in every way, we can flee from him. And if all else fails, just play dead until they leave.

Sun Tzu advises that if your forces are evenly matched with your enemy, you should just go ahead and fight them, like when you finally face off against that one friend in a video game who's always beaten you before. If your enemy has more troops, you should avoid them, like when you walk around the other side of the mall to avoid that one person you don't want to see. And if the odds are just too much against you, you should run away, like when you try to escape from your ex's new partner at a party.

10. Hence, though an obstinate fight may be made by a small force, in the end it must be captured by the larger force. Just like in the corporate world, bigger companies tend to swallow up smaller ones.

Sun Tzu recognizes that a small force may be able to hold out in an obstinate fight, but in the end, it will likely be captured by a larger force. This is a reminder that strength in numbers can often win the day, and that a smaller force must use tactics and strategy to overcome their disadvantage. In modern times, this could mean that smaller businesses or individuals may need to find creative ways to compete with larger entities.

11. Now the general is the bulwark of the State; if the bulwark is complete at all points; the State will be strong; if the bulwark is defective, the State will be weak. And if the general is spending all his time scrolling through social media instead of strategizing, the State is doomed.

The general is like the captain of a ship. If they're doing their job well and making good decisions, the ship (or in this case, the state) will stay afloat. But if the captain is drunk and steering the ship into rocks, well, things aren't going to end well. It's like having a boss who's always slacking off and making bad choices for the company. It's not going to be long before the whole thing falls apart.

Moving on…..

12. Listen up, rulers! There are three major ways you can totally screw up your army:

(1) If you tell your soldiers to move forward or backward without realizing that they can't actually do it, you're hobbling your army.

(2) If you try to run your army like it's a kingdom, you'll just make your soldiers restless and paranoid. Don't be that guy.

(3) If you put the wrong people in charge without considering the situation, your soldiers will lose confidence in your leadership.

Real-life example: Imagine a boss who tells their team to work overnight to meet an impossible deadline, then gets mad when the team can't deliver. Or a boss who tries to micromanage every detail of a project and makes everyone stressed and unhappy. Or a boss who hires a bunch of people without considering their qualifications, leading to a team of unmotivated and unproductive employees. Don't be that boss.

Opinion: The key to being a good leader is to understand your team's strengths and limitations and work with them to achieve your goals. Don't set impossible tasks, don't try to manage your team like they're all the same, and don't hire people without considering their qualifications. Be smart, adaptable, and understanding, and your team will thank you for it.

13. And when your army is restless and paranoid, the other guys will totally take advantage of you. You'll be flinging victory away faster than a hot potato.

If your army is restless and distrustful, it's like adding chaos to an already chaotic situation. It's like trying to herd cats, or trying to organize a group of teenagers to clean their rooms. It's just not going to work, and it's only going to lead to trouble.

Real-life example: Imagine you're a manager trying to lead a team of employees, but your team is constantly bickering and arguing. This creates an environment of distrust and hostility, which can lead to decreased productivity and missed deadlines. It's important to address the underlying issues causing the unrest and work to create a more harmonious work environment.

Opinion: In any group, whether it's an army or a team of employees, it's important to foster an atmosphere of trust and respect. Without this, it's hard to accomplish anything meaningful.

14. So, if you want to win, you gotta remember these five things:

(1) You gotta know when to fight and when to back off.

(2) You gotta be able to handle any kind of force, even if they're way better or way worse than you.

(3) Your whole army needs to be on the same page, working together and not bickering like a bunch of school kids.

(4) Be prepared, but don't jump the gun. Wait for the right moment to strike.

(5) And most importantly, don't let your boss interfere with your military strategy. You're the boss here!

And hey, there's a saying that goes: If you know yourself and your enemy, you're basically unbeatable. If you only know yourself, you'll win some and lose some. But if you know nothing at all, you're pretty much screwed.

Real-life example: Let's say you're a small business owner trying to compete with a larger corporation. In order to win, you need to be strategic in your approach. You need to know when to take risks and when to play it safe. You need to understand your strengths and weaknesses, and how to leverage them to your advantage. You also need to make sure your team is motivated and working together towards a common goal. Finally, you need to be prepared to seize opportunities when they arise.

Opinion: These five essentials are not just important in military strategy, but in any competitive environment. Whether you're running a business, playing sports, or engaging in any other type of competition, understanding these principles can give you a significant advantage.

IV. Tactical Dispositions

1. Yo, Sun Tzu was like: "Back in the day, the badass warriors first made themselves indestructible, and then waited for the perfect opportunity to crush their enemies."

Basically, Sun Tzu is saying that good fighters make sure they're as prepared as possible before going into battle. They eliminate any chance of being defeated and then wait for the right moment to strike. It's like going into a job interview - you want to make sure you're as ready as possible before you even walk through the door.

2. Avoiding defeat is all about your own skills and strategy, but the chance to beat your enemy comes from their own stupidity.

This one is all about being proactive versus reactive. Sun Tzu is saying that it's up to us to make sure we don't lose, but it's the enemy's actions that will give us the opportunity to win. It's like a game of chess

- you can control your own moves, but you have to wait for your opponent to make a mistake before you can capitalize on it.

3. So basically, you can protect yourself from losing, but you can't guarantee that you'll come out on top.

This one is a bit more philosophical. Sun Tzu is saying that even if you do everything right, there's no guarantee you'll win. Sometimes things just don't go your way. But if you prepare properly, at least you'll have a better chance of success.

4. That's why they say, "You can talk the talk, but can you walk the walk?"

Sun Tzu is emphasizing the difference between knowing what to do and actually being able to do it. It's like knowing how to ride a bike, but not actually being able to balance on two wheels. It takes practice and skill to turn knowledge into action.

5. If you want to avoid getting your butt kicked, play defense. But if you want to be the one doing the butt-kicking, you gotta go on the offensive.

If you want to defend yourself, you need to focus on defense. If you want to win, you need to focus on offense. It's like in a football game - if you're ahead, you might switch to a more defensive strategy to protect your lead. But if you're behind, you'll need to take more risks and be more aggressive to try and catch up.

6. Staying on the defense means you ain't got enough muscle. Attacking means you got power to spare.

Sun Tzu is saying that being on the defensive is a sign of weakness, while attacking shows strength. It's like being on the playground - if you're always backing away from the bully, they're going to think you're weak and keep coming after you. But if you stand up to them and fight back, they might back down.

7. A smart general knows how to hide and defend like a ninja, but also knows how to come out of nowhere and dominate like a god. That's how you get the best of both worlds.

Sun Tzu is painting a vivid picture here - the general who is good at defense is like a ninja hiding in the shadows, while the general who is good at offense is like a thunderbolt striking from the sky. But ultimately, the best generals are able to balance both defense and offense. It's like playing a game of Risk - you need to protect your own territories while also expanding into enemy territory.

8. If you can only see victory when it's staring you right in the face, you're not exactly a genius.

Being a great leader means being able to see beyond what the average person sees. If you only see things in the same way as everyone else, then you're not really a great leader. Great leaders can see opportunities that others can't, and they know how to take advantage of them. It's like seeing a hidden door that everyone else has missed. Only the best leaders can find and use that door to their advantage.

9. And it's not really impressive if you win a battle and everyone's like, "Good job, bro."

Winning isn't everything, and true excellence goes beyond just achieving a victory. It's about the process, the strategy, and the skill it takes to come out on top. Just because everyone thinks you're amazing for winning a fight doesn't necessarily mean you're the best fighter out there.

This is a reminder that popularity and public opinion don't always reflect true excellence or mastery. Sometimes, those who are truly skilled and successful might not be as well-known or celebrated.

Example: In the world of sports, there are many athletes who are extremely talented and successful but may not receive as much recognition or praise as others who are more popular or have better marketing strategies.

10. Being able to do easy stuff doesn't mean you're strong. Seeing stuff that's right in front of you doesn't mean you're sharp. And hearing loud noises doesn't mean you got great ears.

Small and easy things are not a measure of great skill or ability.

Opinion: Sun Tzu is emphasizing that true strength and ability are not measured by simple or obvious actions. Rather, they are demonstrated through more complex and difficult challenges.

Example: In the workplace, completing easy tasks or simply showing up to work every day is not enough to prove your worth or skill. It's important to take on challenging projects and demonstrate your abilities through your work.

11. True skill is when you not only win, but make it look like a freakin' cakewalk.

It's not just about the outcome, but the way you get there. Strive to be excellent in everything you do, and don't settle for just getting by. A truly skilled fighter is someone who not only wins, but makes it look easy.

Opinion: This is a reminder that true skill is not just about winning, but about making winning look effortless. It takes a lot of hard work and practice to make something difficult seem easy.
Example: In the entertainment industry, actors who make difficult roles look easy are often considered the most talented. It's not just about memorizing lines, but about making the character come to life in a natural and believable way.

12. And that's the thing - when you're that good, people don't even realize how awesome you are. They just know they don't wanna mess with you.
13. The key to winning battles is to avoid making mistakes. It's like playing tic-tac-toe against a toddler - as long as you don't mess up, you'll win every time.

Being strategic and avoiding mistakes can be just as important as being aggressive and taking risks. Sometimes, the best offense is a good defense.

14. So the savvy warrior puts themselves in a position where defeat is as unlikely as seeing a unicorn on the subway. And they don't wait until the enemy is already dead on the ground to deliver the final blow.

A skilled fighter puts themselves in a position where they cannot be defeated and seizes the opportunity to defeat their opponent.Preparation, strategy, and timing are key to success in any endeavor. Don't wait for opportunities to come to you - create them yourself, and be ready to pounce when the time is right.

15. In war, the winning strategist only fights when they know they've already won. The losing strategist, on the other hand, fights first and then hopes for the best. It's like playing poker with your rent money when you're already down to your last dollar.

This one is all about timing. A smart strategist doesn't rush into battle until they know they've already won. On the other hand, a foolish leader charges into battle hoping for a win, without first securing the victory. It's like someone who celebrates their victory before actually crossing the finish line, versus someone who crosses the finish line first and then celebrates.

A wise leader will only engage in battle once they have secured a victory in some other way, such as through strategic alliances or resource acquisition. In contrast, a doomed leader will jump straight into battle in the hopes of achieving victory without properly preparing.

Example: A modern example of this would be the business world, where a successful company will often build a strong foundation before expanding or making risky investments, while a failing company may try to cut corners or take shortcuts in the hopes of making a quick profit.

Opinion: This emphasizes the importance of patience and strategy in achieving success, which is a lesson that can be applied to many areas of life. It is often better to take time to build a solid foundation before pursuing big goals.

16. The greatest leader upholds moral standards and sticks to a game plan. That way, they're in control of their own success. It's like running a marathon - if you stick to your training and don't stop to eat a dozen donuts halfway through, you'll have a better chance of crossing the finish line.

This emphasizes the importance of a leader's character and ethics in achieving success. A good leader must maintain strict discipline and adhere to a code of morality, which will allow them to better control and direct the outcome of their endeavors.

Example: In a modern context, this can be applied to leaders in politics, business, and other fields. Leaders who are ethical, disciplined, and committed to a set of values tend to inspire trust and respect among their followers, which can lead to more success in the long run.

Opinion: This emphasizes the importance of ethical leadership and integrity, which is a lesson that is particularly relevant in today's world where many leaders have been criticized for their lack of moral character and poor decision-making.

17. When it comes to military strategy, you need to measure your opponent up like a tailor taking your measurements. Then you estimate how many punches it'll take to knock them out. After that, you calculate the odds of victory like you're counting cards in Vegas. Then you balance the risks and rewards, like deciding whether to invest in Bitcoin or Dogecoin. And finally, you aim for the win like a kid trying to dunk on a Fisher-Price hoop.

This outlines the five essential elements required for military victory. These elements are measurement (assessing the situation), estimation of quantity (determining the available resources), calculation (planning and strategy), balancing of chances (weighing the risks and rewards), and finally, victory. This can be applied not only to military strategy but to any endeavor that requires planning and preparation, such as business or sports.
Opinion: This highlights the importance of preparation and strategy in achieving success. It is essential to assess the situation, consider available resources, and plan and strategize before taking action.

18. It's all about balance, like a circus performer walking a tightrope. You need to measure your moves, estimate the risks, calculate your chances, and balance it all out to achieve victory.

This describes the interconnected nature of the five essential elements required for military victory. Each element builds on the previous one, with victory being the ultimate goal.
This can be applied to many areas of life, where success often requires a combination of planning, strategy, and risk-taking.
Opinion: This emphasizes the importance of a holistic approach to achieving success, where each step builds on the previous one. It is essential to take a systematic and thoughtful approach to achieve the desired outcome.

19. When your army is winning, it's like having a pound of chocolate in one hand and a single Skittle in the other - it's not even a fair fight.

Imagine a game of tug-of-war where one team has twice as many people as the other team. Who do you think is going to win? Obviously, the team with more people is going to win because they have a stronger force. The same goes for armies. A victorious army is so much stronger than a defeated one that it's like comparing a fully charged battery to a dead one. It's always better to be on the winning side, right?
In my opinion, this emphasizes the importance of winning in a war. It shows that once an army has won, it becomes incredibly strong and

difficult to defeat. It's better to be the victor than the defeated because it gives you an advantage in future battles.

20. And when you charge into battle with all the force of a herd of wild elephants, it's like unleashing a tidal wave of pure awesome. The enemy won't know what hit 'em.

When an army is conquering, it's like a force of nature that cannot be stopped. It's like a tsunami that crashes into the shore, unstoppable and devastating. Just like how a tsunami can wipe out everything in its path, a conquering army can do the same. The sheer force of a conquering army is unstoppable.

This highlights the power of a conquering army. It shows that once an army starts winning battles, it becomes incredibly strong and unstoppable. This is why it's important to stop an army before it starts conquering because once it gains momentum, it becomes much harder to stop.

Overall, Sun Tzu's teachings emphasize the importance of timing, discipline, strategy, and overwhelming force. A good leader must know when to strike, enforce discipline, and create a strategy that is unstoppable. Sun Tzu's lessons can be applied not just to warfare, but also to everyday life and business.

V. Energy

1. Leading a big group of people is just like leading your small group of friends. It's all about finding the right balance and divvying up the tasks.

      In modern terms, this means that whether you're leading a small team or a massive organization, effective leadership means breaking down the group into manageable units. This could mean assigning different people to specific tasks or dividing the team into smaller groups that can work independently. Managing a group of people is like trying to control a pack of hungry wolves - you need to make sure they don't turn on each other and start fighting. So, break them down into smaller groups and assign each one a specific task. That way, they'll work together like a pack of loyal puppies instead of a bunch of snarling wolves.

2. Having a massive squad at your disposal isn't all that different from having a small team, except you'll need some serious hand signals and secret codes.

      Have you ever tried to coordinate a group project where everyone was doing their own thing? It's like herding cats! That's why you need clear signs and signals to keep everyone on the same page. It's like a game of charades, but with tanks and guns.

3. If you want your squad to be tough as nails and impervious to enemy attacks, you gotta be a master of both direct and sneaky maneuvers.

To withstand the enemy's attack, you need to be prepared and use both direct and indirect tactics. It's like being in a snowball fight. You can either stand there and take it, or you can dodge and weave like a ninja. Sometimes, you need to hit the enemy head-on (direct) and other times, you need to be sneaky and hit them where they least expect it (indirect). Just make sure you don't accidentally hit your own team!

4. To really wreck your enemies and make them look like a breakfast omelet, you gotta know all about their weak spots and how to hit 'em where it hurts.

You want your army to have a powerful impact against the enemy, which requires knowledge of weak points and strong points. Think of it like playing a game of Jenga. You need to know which blocks are weak and which ones are strong to build a sturdy tower. Same goes for the army - you need to know which points to attack (weak) and which ones to defend (strong) to come out on top. Just make sure your tower doesn't topple over!

5. Sometimes you gotta go head-to-head with your enemy, but most of the time you gotta be sneakier than a cat burglar to come out on top.

Sometimes you need to use direct tactics to engage in battle, but you also need to use indirect tactics to secure victory. It's like a game of dodgeball. You need to charge into battle and pelt the enemy with balls (direct), but you also need to use tactics like hiding behind obstacles or faking out your opponent (indirect) to win the game. Just make sure you don't get hit in the face!

6. Indirect tactics are like your favorite TV show - they seem to go on forever, never losing their touch, like a never-ending stream or a new season of Stranger Things.

    Indirect tactics can be used endlessly and are like the cycles of nature.

7. It's crazy to think that there are only five musical notes, but the combinations and remixes of those notes can create more bangers than your Spotify playlist could ever handle.

    Sun Tzu is saying that just like there are only five musical notes, but they can be combined in endless ways to create different melodies, there are only a few basic principles in warfare, but they can be applied in countless ways to achieve victory.

8. Just like there are only five primary colors, there are only so many ways to mix and match them to create infinite shades. It's the same in war, whether you have a small army or a big one, it's all about how you use what you have.

    Sun Tzu points out that the primary colors are limited, but when combined, they create an infinite spectrum of hues. In the same way, basic military tactics may be few in number, but they can be combined in endless ways to outmaneuver an enemy. It's like mixing drinks at a party: you might only have vodka, soda, and lime juice, but you can make so many different cocktails that your friends will never want to leave.

9. There are only five basic tastes, but mix them up and you can create a flavor explosion. In war, you only have two options: direct attack or indirect tactics. But when you combine them, you get a feast of strategies that will keep your enemy guessing.

10. Think of war as a mix between painting and cooking. You only have so many colors or flavors to work with, but it's all about how you blend them together to create something new and unexpected.

11. When it comes to attacking, there are only so many ways to do it directly or indirectly. But the beauty of war is that you can keep combining these methods to create endless possibilities. It's like a never-ending dance where each move leads to the next.

12. Troops charging into battle are like a raging river, unstoppable and fierce. But just like a river can carry rocks along its path, so can an army use its force to crush its enemies.

     Sun Tzu is emphasizing the importance of a strong and forceful attack that can overwhelm an enemy. It's like a football team making a strong push down the field, knocking over anyone in their way.

13. Making the right decision in war is like a falcon swooping down to catch its prey at the perfect moment. It takes skill and precision to know when to strike and when to hold back.

Making a decision is like a falcon swooping in on its prey. If you hesitate or swoop too late, you'll miss your target and end up feeling pretty foolish. This is a reminder that decision-making is crucial in life. It's important to trust your instincts and act decisively when you need to. However, it's also important to take your time and consider your options before making a final decision.

14. A good fighter knows how to strike fear into the heart of their enemy, and when the time comes, they don't hesitate. It's like pulling the trigger on a crossbow – once you let go, there's no turning back.

This emphasizes the importance of both aggression and decisiveness in battle. A fighter who is hesitant or timid will not be successful.

15. Energy in war is like bending a crossbow, storing up power until the right moment. But when that moment comes, decision-making is like releasing the trigger, unleashing all that energy in one swift action.

Imagine you're an archer aiming at a target. You need to use your energy to bend the bow and then make a quick decision about when to release the arrow. This emphasizes the importance of both physical and mental preparation in achieving your goals. You need to have the energy and strength to work towards your goals, but you also need to make smart decisions and take action when the time is right.

16. In the chaos of battle, it may seem like there's no order, but a well-disciplined army can turn seeming disorder into an advantage. Like a

flock of birds or a school of fish, they move as one, even without a clear leader.

In modern terms, this passage is saying that even when things look chaotic and disorganized, they can still be effective. In a battle, for example, it may look like everyone is running around randomly, but in reality, they're following a plan that's been carefully crafted ahead of time. This passage is reminding us not to judge a book by its cover, and to remember that things aren't always what they seem.

17. Sometimes, in war, you have to fake it to make it. Simulating disorder can actually be a sign of perfect discipline, simulated fear can show courage, and simulated weakness can reveal strength. It's all about using psychology to your advantage.

18. Putting a neat and tidy front on chaos is just a matter of breaking it down into smaller pieces. Making cowardice look like shyness takes some serious underlying courage. And tricking your enemy by pretending to be weak is all about tactical maneuvers, baby.

Sometimes it can be effective to pretend to be something you're not. For example, if you're in a fight and you act like you're scared, your opponent might lower their guard, thinking they have the upper hand. But if you suddenly attack them with all your strength, they'll be caught off guard and you'll be more likely to win. This is a strategy called "feigning weakness to gain strength."

19. If you wanna keep your enemy guessing, you gotta be sneaky. You make 'em think you're gonna do one thing, but then you do another.

And maybe sacrifice a little something along the way, just to keep 'em interested.

This is about the importance of keeping your opponent off balance. If you can make it seem like you're giving up something valuable or leaving yourself vulnerable, your opponent might take the bait and attack. But if you're prepared for their attack, you can turn the tables and defeat them. This is another strategy that involves deception and misdirection.

20. Keep 'em moving, keep 'em guessing, that's the name of the game. Dangle a carrot in front of 'em and watch 'em chase after it. Then, when they least expect it, you hit 'em with your best shot.

You can lure your opponent into chasing after something that seems valuable, you can then ambush them with a more powerful force. This is a classic tactic in guerrilla warfare, where smaller groups use deception and surprise to defeat larger, more organized armies. This strategy requires patience and cunning, as the fighter needs to wait for the right moment to strike. It can also be risky, as the opponent may catch on to the ruse and turn the tables.

21. It's all about teamwork, man. You can't expect one person to do it all. You gotta find the right people for the job and bring 'em together. And when you do, watch out, 'cause they're gonna be unstoppable.

The smart fighter knows that teamwork makes the dream work. He carefully selects the best fighters with complementary skills and personalities, like a fantasy football draft. He then coordinates their attacks to create a force greater than the sum of its parts, like the Power Rangers. This passage emphasizes the importance of teamwork and leadership in achieving victory. It also highlights the need to recognize and utilize individual strengths to benefit the group as a whole.

22. When your team is firing on all cylinders, they're like a bunch of rolling stones, man. Nothing can stop 'em. They'll mow down anything in their path, just like a round stone rolling down a hill.

23. That energy, man, it's like a force of nature. It's like a boulder rolling down a mountain, picking up speed and power as it goes. And when you harness that energy, there's nothing you can't do.

Remember, it's all about teamwork. Use your combined energy to roll over your enemies like round stones down a mountain. Boom, that's how you win at war, Sun Tzu style!"

VI. Weak Points and Strong

1. Sun Tzu said: If you're the first to arrive on the battlefield, you'll be feeling fresh and ready for action. But if you're the second, you'll be exhausted from all that running.

It's like being the first one to show up to a party. You're fresh, you're ready to go, and you can handle anything that comes your way.

But if you're the last one to arrive, you're gonna be tired, sweaty, and everyone's gonna be looking at you like, "Dude, where have you been?"

2. So, the smart fighter makes sure he's in control of the situation, and doesn't let the enemy call the shots.

    This is like playing a game of chess. You want to be in control of the board and make your opponent react to your moves, rather than the other way around. Sun Tzu is saying that a smart fighter will take charge of the situation and dictate the terms of the battle, rather than being at the mercy of their opponent's actions.

3. He can lure the enemy in with enticing advantages, or inflict damage to prevent them from getting too close.

    This is like dangling a carrot in front of someone to get them to follow you, or using a stick to keep them away. Sun Tzu is saying that by offering incentives or causing damage, a fighter can either lure their enemy into a trap or keep them at a safe distance.

4. If the enemy is lounging around, give them a little poke. If they have food to spare, starve them out. If they're comfortably settled, make them pack up and move.

    This is like teasing your little brother while he's playing video games, or hiding the snacks so he can't eat them. Sun Tzu is saying that by disrupting their opponent's comfort, supply, or location, a fighter can weaken them and gain an advantage.

5. Pop up where the enemy least expects you, and move fast to get there.

This is like jumping out from behind a corner to scare someone, or sneaking up on a friend when they least expect it. Sun Tzu is saying that by attacking from unexpected angles or places, a fighter can catch their opponent off guard and gain the upper hand.

6. An army can travel great distances without any trouble, as long as they're not travelling through enemy territory.

It's all about avoiding unnecessary drama. If you know there's gonna be trouble in a certain area, you gotta steer clear of it. It's like taking the scenic route to avoid rush hour traffic. It might take a little longer, but you'll get there without all the stress.

7. Attack where there's no defense, and defend where there's no attack.

This is like robbing an empty house versus trying to rob a bank with armed guards. Sun Tzu is saying that by targeting weak points and defending strong ones, a fighter can maximize their chances of success and minimize their chances of failure.

8. The art of war is all about keeping your enemy guessing. Attack where they don't expect it, and defend where they're not looking.

A skilled general should be able to find and exploit their enemy's weaknesses. If the opponent doesn't know where to defend or what to attack, then they will be at a disadvantage. This applies not only to physical warfare but also to business competition, where a successful company can find the weak spots of their rivals and exploit them to gain an advantage.

9. Oh, the glorious art of sneakiness and secrecy! With your help, we can be invisible and inaudible, holding the enemy's fate in our crafty little hands.

    It is all about the power of secrecy and deception in warfare. Being invisible and inaudible allows you to control the situation without the enemy even knowing you're there. It's like the ultimate game of hide and seek, where the stakes are life and death. In today's world, this might look like hacking into your enemy's computer systems and stealing their secrets or sending in spies to gather intel. By being invisible and inaudible, you can control the enemy's fate without them even knowing it. It's like being a ninja in the digital age.

10. Want to be a force to be reckoned with? Find your enemy's weaknesses and exploit them. Want to make a quick escape? Just move faster than the guy chasing you.

    It's like a game of cat and mouse, where the cat is the attacker and the mouse is the defender. Being able to identify and target the enemy's weak points is a key strategy for success. If you can hit their vulnerabilities hard and fast, you'll be able to achieve your objectives more easily. By being faster and smarter than your enemy, you can gain the upper hand and avoid getting caught.

11. Don't let a little thing like a giant wall or a deep ditch stop you from taking on your enemy. Attack somewhere else and watch them scramble to keep up.

     Sun Tzu is advocating for a strategy of deception in this passage. If you can make the enemy think you're attacking one area, they'll be forced to defend it, leaving other areas vulnerable. This is a strategy that has been used in many different types of conflicts, from physical warfare to political campaigning.

12. If you're not in the mood for a fight, just mess with your enemy's head. Throw something weird at them and watch them freak out.

     Sometimes the best way to avoid a fight is to confuse the enemy. If they can't figure out what you're doing, they'll be less likely to engage with you. It's like playing a game of poker and bluffing your way to victory. Or like when you're in a heated argument and you throw them off by changing the subject or doing something unexpected.

13. Want to keep your troops together while your enemy splits up? Find out what your enemy's up to without letting them know you're watching.

     "Know thy enemy" is the first rule of warfare, but sometimes it's even better to keep your own plans hidden. By doing so, you can force your enemy to spread out their forces and make themselves vulnerable to your concentrated attack. It's like playing a game of hide-and-seek, except the stakes are higher and the consequences are more serious.

For example, a hacker who can remain invisible while infiltrating a computer system can cause much more damage than one who is easily detected.

14. When you're united and your enemy's divided, you've got the upper hand. It's like a whole pack of wolves versus a few lost puppies.

When you're facing a larger enemy, it's important to stick together and present a united front. This makes it harder for the enemy to pick you off one by one. In contrast, if the enemy is divided into smaller factions, they become easier targets. It's like a group project in school: if everyone works together, the project will be stronger than if each person does their own thing. But if some members of the group don't cooperate, the project will suffer.

15. When you've got more troops than your enemy, you're in a great position to kick their butts. It's just basic math, people.

If you have a superior force, you have a major advantage in battle. You can use this to attack the enemy's weaker areas and put them in a tight spot. It's like a game of tug-of-war: if one side is much stronger than the other, they will easily win the game. In a real-life example, a company with a better marketing budget and strategy can easily outcompete a smaller business.

16. Keep your battle plans under wraps and your enemy will be too busy preparing for every possibility to focus on any one point. They'll be spread so thin, you'll barely have to lift a finger.

It's important to keep your battle plans secret, so that the enemy can't prepare against you. If they have to spread their forces out to defend multiple points, they will be weaker at any one point. It's like a surprise party: if the guest of honor knows about the party ahead of time, they can prepare themselves and won't be as surprised. But if the party is a secret, they won't know what's coming and will be caught off guard.

17. When your enemy tries to strengthen one area, they'll weaken another. It's like trying to plug a bunch of holes in a leaky boat. Good luck with that.

If the enemy strengthens one area, they will weaken another. This means that they have to make trade-offs and can't be strong everywhere. It's like a game of Jenga: if you pull out one block to strengthen the tower, another part of the tower will become weaker. In business, if a company focuses too much on one product or service, they may neglect other important areas of their business.

18. When you force your enemy to prepare for every possible attack, they'll end up being weak in all areas. It's like trying to be good at everything but ending up being mediocre at everything.

If you can force your adversary to prepare for your attacks, you have the advantage of numerical strength. This means that they have to spend resources to defend against you, while you can use your resources more efficiently. It's like a game of chess: if you can force your opponent to move their pieces in certain ways, you can gain an advantage and eventually win the game. In the business world, a company that can force its competitors to spend more money on marketing or R&D will have a stronger position in the market.

19. Got a big battle coming up? No problem. Just round up your troops from far and wide and get ready to rumble.

Sun Tzu was a master of logistics. He knew that knowing the place and time of battle was essential for winning. If you know when and where the fight is happening, you can concentrate your forces and strike with maximum impact.

20. If we don't know when and where we'll fight, we might as well be a bunch of ants scattering in different directions. Even the ants closer to each other won't be able to help out! And forget about the ones further away, they might as well be on another planet!

On the other hand, if you don't know when or where the battle is happening, things get messy. You can't coordinate your forces effectively, and everyone is left to fend for themselves.

21. Even if the enemy has more soldiers than us, we'll still kick their butts. I mean, who cares about numbers when you have swagger?

Sun Tzu was confident that victory could be achieved, even if the enemy had more soldiers. It's all about strategy and tactics. You can use surprise attacks, psychological warfare, or other methods to gain an advantage. It's like a game of poker: even if your opponent has a better hand, you can still win by bluffing or using other techniques.

22. Don't let the enemy fight us just because they have more soldiers. Snoop around, find out their plans, and see if they're even worth fighting.

If you're facing a stronger enemy, it's important to prevent them from fighting. This means disrupting their plans and preventing them from using their full strength.

23. Get the enemy riled up and see what they're made of. Then we'll know exactly where to hit them where it hurts.

To defeat your enemy, you need to know their strengths and weaknesses. This means studying their behavior and forcing them to reveal their vulnerabilities. It's like playing a game of "Truth or Dare" with your opponent: if you can get them to reveal their secrets, you can use that information to gain an advantage.

24. Study the enemy like you're cramming for a test. Know where you're weak and where you're strong, so you don't end up being the weak link.

To win a battle, you need to know your strengths and weaknesses compared to the enemy's. It's like playing a game of "rock, paper, scissors" and figuring out which moves your opponent is likely to make. If you know their tendencies, you can exploit them and win more often.

25. Keep our tactics hidden like a secret recipe. No one, not even the smartest of the smart, will be able to crack it.

Concealment is key to successful tactics, keeping your plans secret makes it harder for your enemy to anticipate your moves and counter them. It's like keeping your cards close to your chest in a game of poker: if you don't show your hand, your opponents won't know what you're planning.

26. We'll win by using the enemy's own tactics against them. It's like giving them a taste of their own medicine, but instead of medicine, it's a beating.

27. Anyone can see how we're gonna win the battle, but what they won't see is how we got there. We'll make victory look like a piece of cake.

Sun Tzu was a strategist as well as a tactician. He knew that winning a battle was not just about using the right tactics, but also about having a larger strategy in mind. It's like building a house: you need to have a clear vision of what you want to achieve, as well as a plan for how to get there.

28. Don't just use the same tactics over and over again like a broken record. Change it up depending on the situation, like a DJ mixing beats.

Sun Tzu warns against being too rigid in your tactics. What worked once may not work again in different circumstances. It's important to be flexible and adapt your tactics to the situation at hand. It's like trying to catch a fish: you need to change your bait and approach depending on the type of fish and the conditions of the water.

29. Military tactics are like water, they flow to the lowest point. In war, we'll avoid the strong points and hit the weak ones like a boxer targeting the body.

Military tactics are fluid, like water. You need to be able to adapt and change course depending on the terrain and the conditions. It's like a river: it flows around obstacles and takes the path of least resistance, always moving forward towards its goal.

30. Just like water, we'll adapt to the ground we're fighting on. We'll take on the enemy based on their strengths and weaknesses, like a chameleon blending in with its surroundings.

Sun Tzu compared military tactics to water. Water always seeks the path of least resistance, and military tactics should do the same. It's like trying to navigate a crowded dance floor: you need to be nimble and adapt to the movements of the other dancers.

31. Water doesn't have a set path, it flows based on what's in its way. Same goes for us, we'll fight based on who we're facing. We'll adapt like water and flow around our enemy.

32. In war, things can change in a blink of an eye. We'll adapt to anything the enemy throws at us, like a surfer riding the waves.

33. If you can switch up your tactics depending on your opponent and still come out on top, then you're a total boss.

A true master of warfare knows that there is no one-size-fits-all approach. Just like how your mom has to adjust her cooking when she's catering to your picky aunt's taste buds, a great general must adapt their tactics to suit their opponent.

34. The elements (water, fire, wood, metal, earth) don't always play fair, and neither do the seasons. Sometimes things are short, sometimes they're long, and the moon can't make up its mind whether it's coming or going.

The elements of water, fire, wood, metal, and earth all have their strengths and weaknesses, just like the different types of Pokemon. A savvy general will know which element to use to their advantage depending on the situation. And just like how the weather changes with the seasons, a good general needs to be aware of how the environment can affect their battle plans.

VII. Maneuvering

1. Sun Tzu was like, in war, the general takes orders from the big boss.

Sun Tzu is reminding us that in war, the general must ultimately answer to a higher authority. In modern times, this could be the government or the people who have elected them. Even the most skilled general cannot act without the support and direction of those above them.

2. First, get your army together and make sure everyone gets along before you set up camp.

Before any tactical maneuvering can begin, the general must first ensure that their army is unified and working together as a cohesive unit. In modern times, this means that the general must ensure that their troops have the necessary equipment, training, and support to carry out their mission. Without this foundation, even the most brilliant tactical maneuver will fail.

3. Then comes the hard part: tactical maneuvering. It's all about turning the tricky stuff into the straightforward, and making the bad stuff work in your favor.

Tactical maneuvering is one of the most difficult aspects of warfare. It requires the ability to adapt and change course quickly in response to the enemy's movements. Sun Tzu emphasizes the importance of turning a disadvantage into an advantage - in modern times, this means that a general must be able to turn a setback into an opportunity.

4. For example, take the long way around to lure the enemy out of position, then hustle to beat them to the prize. That's some sneaky smarts right there.

Sun Tzu is describing a tactic known as the "indirect approach." By taking a longer route and deceiving the enemy, a general can gain an advantage and arrive at the objective before the enemy does. In modern times, this could be seen as a form of misdirection or distraction.

5. It's way better to maneuver with a well-trained army than a bunch of random folks off the street. Trust us on this one.

      Having a well-trained army is crucial. An undisciplined mob can be more of a liability than an asset.

6. Sending out a whole army to get the job done might not always work out. Sometimes, you gotta send a small group to do the dirty work, even if it means sacrificing their snacks and gear. It's like sending your most trusted friend to do a dangerous job, but they come back with the reward.

      The general must strike a balance between speed and efficiency. Sending a fully equipped army on a march may be too slow to catch the enemy, but detaching a small group may result in a loss of resources. In modern times, this highlights the importance of logistics and supply chains, which can determine the success or failure of a military campaign.

7. If you tell your soldiers to march non-stop, day and night, to get the upper hand, you're gonna lose some leaders along the way. It's like running a marathon, but instead of getting a medal, you get captured.

      Basically, if you try to push your soldiers too hard, they'll get tired and fall behind, and your enemies will swoop in and capture your leaders. It's like when you're playing a game of Capture the Flag, and you make a break for the enemy's base, but you run out of steam halfway there and get tagged by their sneaky ninja player.

8. If you don't plan your march right, you're gonna have some soldiers lagging behind and getting tired. You'll only end up with a fraction of your army at the finish line. It's like trying to run a race, but only a few people actually make it to the end.

So, if you want to avoid that scenario, you can't just rely on the strongest soldiers to lead the way. You need to pace yourself and make sure everyone can keep up. It's like when you're on a road trip and you're trying to get to your destination as fast as possible, but your friend in the backseat needs to stop for a bathroom break every hour.

9. Only the strongest will survive, and that's not a good look for your army.
10. But if you cut that distance in half, you'll still lose a third of your troops.

So, the key is to find the right balance between speed and sustainability. You want to make progress, but you also want to make sure your army is well-fed and well-rested.

11. Basically, if you don't have supplies and a solid base, you're gonna lose.

And speaking of being well-fed, you can't forget about your supply chain. If you don't have enough food and equipment, your army is pretty much doomed.

12. You can't form alliances until you know what your neighbors are up to. It's just common sense.

    You can't just jump into alliances with your neighbors without knowing what they're up to. It's like when you're deciding whether to team up with someone for a group project, but you don't know if they're going to do their fair share of the work or slack off and leave you hanging.

13. And you can't lead an army unless you know the lay of the land. Mountains, forests, swamps - you gotta know it all.

    You can't be a good navigator if you're relying solely on Google Maps. Get to know the lay of the land if you want to lead a successful road trip. Knowing the terrain you're navigating is essential for any successful journey, whether you're leading an army or just trying to find your way to the nearest Taco Bell.

14. That means getting some local guides who know the area.

    If you want to know where the best tacos are in a new city, ask a local. They know what's up. Local guides can provide valuable insight and help you make the most of your surroundings. Plus, who doesn't love getting insider tips on the best food spots?

15. Bottom line: deception is key to winning. Keep your true plans hidden, and you'll come out on top.

Fake it 'til you make it, baby. This speaks to the importance of strategy and tact in war (and in life). Sometimes, you need to play your cards close to your chest to come out on top.

16. Whether to concentrate your troops or spread them out depends on the situation. Use your head.

Flexibility is key. There's no one right way to approach a situation. You need to be able to adapt to the circumstances at hand and make strategic decisions based on the information available to you.

17. Move fast like the wind, but stay tight like a forest. Got it?

Be swift and agile, but also strong and unyielding. This highlights the importance of balance. You want to be able to move quickly and efficiently, but you also need to be able to hold your ground when necessary.

18. When it's time to raid and plunder, be like a raging fire. But when you need to hold your ground, be like a mountain.

Be like a flame: bendy, but still able to burn your enemies to a crisp. Similar this one emphasizes the importance of balance. You need to be able to adapt to changing circumstances, but also maintain a strong foundation.

19. Keep your plans so secret, they're like a black hole. And when it's time to strike, hit 'em like a bolt of lightning.

Sun Tzu is advocating for some serious sneakiness here. I guess the idea is that if your enemies can't see what you're planning, they won't be able to prepare for it. And then, when you do strike, you should do it with all the force and suddenness of a thunderbolt. I can definitely see the appeal of this approach, especially if you're up against a particularly formidable foe.

20. When you go looting, make sure to spread the wealth among your crew. And if you conquer new land, make sure to cut it up into sweet plots of land for your homies.

Basically, Sun Tzu is saying that if you're going to steal stuff or conquer land, you need to share the wealth with your crew. It's like when you're playing a video game with your friends and you find a bunch of treasure - you don't want to hog it all for yourself, you gotta split it up! This is a pretty decent strategy, since it keeps your soldiers or crew members happy and motivated.

21. Before making your next move, take a hot minute to think and plan it out.

Sun Tzu reminds us to think before we act. This is solid advice, especially in today's fast-paced world where we're constantly being bombarded with information and pressure to make quick decisions. Taking a moment to pause and reflect can help us make better, more strategic choices. Of course, if you're in a Fortnite battle royale, you might not have time to ponder too long, so just use your instincts and hope for the best!

22. The key to victory is being able to swerve and dodge like a boss. That's what maneuvering is all about.

23. The Book of Army Management says: When you're in the heat of battle, yelling can only get you so far. That's why we got gongs and drums, and flags and banners.

24. Gongs, drums, flags, and banners all help to focus your army's attention on one specific objective.

Let's talk about gongs, drums, banners, and flags. These are all important tools that have been used in warfare for centuries to communicate with troops and coordinate movements. But let's be real, in the age of modern technology and communication, do we really need gongs and drums anymore? Maybe we can upgrade to some walkie-talkies or cell phones. And as for banners and flags, I mean, they look cool and all, but they're not exactly the most practical way to communicate important information. Maybe we can invest in some high-tech holographic displays instead.

25. This way, your army will be like one big happy family, and no one can break off and do their own thing. This is how you handle a huge group of people.

Sun Tzu reminds us that a united army is a strong army. When everyone is working together towards a common goal, it's much harder for the enemy to break through and cause chaos. So, let's make sure we're working as a team and supporting each other in our endeavors, whether it's in the battlefield or in our day-to-day lives. Together, we can accomplish great things!

26. When you're fighting in the dark, light up those signal fires and beat those drums. And when it's daytime, wave those flags and banners like you mean it. That's how you influence your army.

Sun Tzu again emphasizes the importance of using different signals to communicate with your army depending on the situation. Signal-fires and drums may be useful in the dark of night, while flags and banners are more visible during the day. But let's be real, in modern warfare, we have much more advanced ways of communicating with our troops. Instead of relying on fires and drums, we can use radios, satellite phones, and other advanced technologies to keep in touch with our soldiers.

27. If an army loses its fighting spirit, or a general loses their cool, then it's game over.

A defeated army is often one that has lost its spirit and its commander has lost their presence of mind. This is why it's important for leaders to maintain a positive attitude and to inspire their troops to stay motivated and focused.

28. Soldiers are most pumped up in the morning, but by noon, they start to slow down. And by evening, they're already thinking about hitting the hay.

Sun Tzu goes on to note that a soldier's spirit is at its highest in the morning, and by evening, they're more focused on getting back to camp than fighting. A clever general will avoid attacking an army when it's at its strongest, but instead wait for the right moment when the army is feeling sluggish and dispirited. This is the art of studying moods and knowing when to strike.

29. A smart general knows to avoid a pumped-up army, but go after them when they're ready to call it quits. That's how you study your enemy's mood.

Sun Tzu reminds us of the importance of remaining calm and disciplined in the face of chaos. A good leader knows how to maintain their composure even when everything around them is falling apart. By remaining calm and disciplined, they can wait for their enemy to reveal their weaknesses and capitalize on them.

30. Stay cool and collected, even when everyone around you is freaking out. That's how you keep your head in the game.

Be a Zen master on the battlefield. When everyone else is losing their minds, you're cool as a cucumber. You wait patiently for the enemy to show their hand, and then you strike. It's all about being disciplined and calm, even in the face of chaos. It's like that old saying: "Keep calm and carry on, even when you're in the middle of a war zone."

31. The key to victory is to conserve your energy. Let the enemy do all the hard work while you sit back and relax. It's like getting through a long day by taking plenty of coffee breaks.

32. Don't attack an enemy when they're all lined up and ready to go. It's like trying to jump into a game of tag when everyone else is already in position.

      This is a tricky one. On the one hand, you don't want to attack an enemy that's well-prepared and ready for you. On the other hand, you don't want to wait too long and let them get the upper hand. It's all about studying your enemy and understanding their strengths and weaknesses. You want to find the right moment to strike - when their guard is down and their banners are in disarray.

33. Don't go uphill against the enemy, and don't attack them when they're coming downhill. It's like trying to climb a mountain while someone else is skiing down.

      It's all about choosing your battles wisely. You don't want to put yourself at a disadvantage by fighting on difficult terrain. Instead, you want to find a place where you have the advantage - maybe a flat field or a narrow pass. It's all about understanding the circumstances and making the most of them.

34. Don't fall for the enemy's tricks. If they're pretending to run away, don't chase after them. And don't mess with soldiers who are feeling feisty. It's like trying to win at poker against a master bluffer.

Don't chase someone who's faking it and don't mess with someone who's clearly not in the mood. This is actually pretty solid advice. It's all about knowing when to strike and when to hold back. It's like when your friend says they're "fine" but you can tell they're clearly upset. Don't push it, just give them some space.

35. Don't take the bait when the enemy offers it. And don't bother attacking an army that's already headed home. It's like trying to catch a fish that's already thrown the hook.

Don't fall for the enemy's tricks and don't mess with someone who's already heading back to their own turf. This one's all about being aware of your surroundings and not getting played. It's like when you get a sketchy email from a "Nigerian prince" offering to give you money. Don't fall for it! And if someone's already leaving, just let them go. No need to stir up more trouble.

36. When you've got an army surrounded, give them a way out. Don't push them too hard, or they might turn on you. It's like trying to corral a bunch of cats.

When you've got someone cornered, don't block off all their escape routes. And don't push someone who's already backed into a corner. Sun Tzu really knows his stuff. If you're in a position of power, you don't need to completely crush your opponent. Just give them a way out so they can save face and retreat. It's like when you're playing a game of Monopoly and your little sister is about to go bankrupt. You don't need to buy all her properties, just let her give up gracefully.

37. That's the art of warfare, folks. It's like playing a really intense game of Risk, but with actual consequences.

Short and sweet. Sun Tzu knows his stuff and he's not afraid to show it.

VIII. Variation in Tactics

1. Sun Tzu was like, "Listen up, generals! You gotta do what the big boss says, get your army together, and focus your energy."

The boss calls the shots, the general gathers the troops, and they all come together to form a powerful army. This one's pretty straightforward. It's all about teamwork and following orders. It's like when you're working on a group project and the teacher assigns a leader. You listen to the leader and work together to get the job done.

2. When you're in a rough neighborhood, don't hang around too long. If there's a crossroads, team up with your buddies. Don't get caught with your pants down. If things get really hairy, bust out some sneaky tactics or just go full-on Rambo.

When the going gets tough, keep moving and don't get stuck in one place. If you're in a good location, team up with your allies. Don't put yourself in dangerous situations and be creative when you're feeling trapped. And if things are really dire, you gotta fight for your life. Sun Tzu is all about adaptability and resourcefulness. When things get rough, you gotta be able to think on your feet and come up with new solutions. It's like when you're lost in the woods and your phone dies. You can't just sit there and wait for help, you gotta keep moving and try to find your way out.

3. There are some roads that are just plain stupid to take, some armies that you just don't mess with, some cities that are just asking for a good old-fashioned siege, some positions that you just gotta give up, and some orders from your boss that you should just straight-up ignore.

 Not everything is fair game in war. There are certain roads, armies, towns, and positions that you should avoid. And sometimes, you gotta question your boss's orders. This is a good reminder that just because you're in a war, doesn't mean you can do whatever you want. There are still rules and boundaries that need to be respected. It's like when you're playing a game of dodgeball and someone's hiding behind the gym equipment. You don't throw the ball at them, that's not fair.

4. If you know how to mix up your moves on the battlefield, you'll be a boss. If you don't, you might as well stay home and watch Netflix.

 If you're a boss who knows how to mix things up, your team will be more effective. Sun Tzu is right on the money with this one. If you're leading a team, it's important to have a few different strategies in your back pocket. If Plan A isn't working, you can switch to Plan B, and so on. That way, you'll always be one step ahead of the competition.

5. You could be a geography genius, but if you don't know how to use that knowledge to your advantage, you're gonna have a bad time.

If you're a boss who doesn't know how to mix things up, your knowledge won't help you much. This one's a bit of a harsh truth, but it's true nonetheless. Even if you know everything there is to know about a situation, if you don't know how to adapt to changing circumstances, you won't get very far.

6. Even if you know all the theory, if you can't put it into practice, you're gonna flop like a fish on dry land.

If you're a boss who doesn't know how to mix things up, you won't be able to get the most out of your team. Sun Tzu really hammers this point home, doesn't he? If you're not willing to be flexible and adaptable, you're not going to be very effective as a leader. It's important to be able to switch gears when the situation calls for it.

7. A good leader takes both the good and the bad into account. If you only focus on the good, you're setting yourself up for disappointment.

Smart bosses weigh the pros and cons of every situation before making a decision. This is just common sense, really. If you're a leader, you need to be able to balance the potential benefits of a course of action with the risks involved. It's all about making informed decisions.

8. If you're not realistic about what you can and can't achieve, you're gonna end up with a lot of egg on your face.

If we're realistic about the potential outcomes of our decisions, we'll be more likely to achieve our goals. Sun Tzu is really just reiterating his previous point here. If you're able to balance the risks and rewards of a decision, you'll be more likely to make the right call. It's all about being pragmatic.

9. When things get tough, don't just sit there like a deer in headlights. Look for opportunities to turn things around.

10. Keep your enemies on their toes by hitting them where it hurts, stirring up trouble, and tempting them with shiny things.

11. Don't assume your enemy won't show up just because they haven't yet. Instead, be ready for anything and make sure your defenses are on point.

12. Sun Tzu warned that a general could mess up in five big ways:
    (1) being reckless and getting their whole army destroyed;
    (2) being a scaredy-cat and getting themselves captured;
    (3) having a short fuse and getting easily triggered by insults;
    (4) being too proud and sensitive to shame; and
    (5) caring too much about their soldiers and getting bogged down in worry and trouble.
Sun Tzu is basically giving a warning to all the wannabe generals out there - don't be an idiot!

There are five major ways you can mess up and get yourself into trouble. First up, we have recklessness - it's like playing Grand Theft Auto and driving off a cliff just for fun. Not smart. Then there's

cowardice - that's like running away from a fight and getting caught by the enemy. No one wants to be that guy. Third, we have a hasty temper - you don't want to be the hothead who gets triggered by every little insult. Fourth, there's "delicacy of honor" - that means you're too worried about your reputation to make good decisions. And finally, there's over-solicitude for your men - that just means you're too busy trying to be everyone's best friend instead of being a strong leader.
Basically, these five sins are like kryptonite to a general's success in war. Avoid them at all costs, folks.

Sun Tzu's warning is still relevant today. Whether you're a military leader or just trying to make it through life, it's important to recognize your weaknesses and work on them. If you're reckless, cowardly, or too sensitive to criticism, you're not going to get very far. And while it's important to care for others, being a pushover can be just as bad as being a tyrant. So, take Sun Tzu's advice and strive to be a strong, confident, and effective leader.

12. If an army falls apart and its leader bites the dust, you can bet your booty that it was due to one of these five deadly sins. So, take some time to reflect on them and don't make the same mistakes, or you'll be toast.

IX. The Army on the March

1. When it comes to setting up camp and spotting the enemy, Sun Tzu says to hurry up and get over the mountains, and hang out near the valleys.

    Sun Tzu was basically saying, "Don't waste your time sightseeing, get to your destination ASAP." But he also added, "Watch out for the enemy, they could be hiding behind that scenic overlook, waiting to ambush you." So, remember to keep your eyes peeled for any suspicious activity, especially if you're on a road trip.

2. Pick a high spot with plenty of sun, but don't go climbing up cliffs to start a battle. That's all you need to know for mountain warfare.

    Ah yes, the joys of camping in high places. The views are great, but don't climb up there just to start a fight. And always face the sun, unless you want to get sunburned and blinded by your own glare.

3. If you've crossed a river, get outta there fast, like you just ate some bad Chinese takeout.

    When crossing a river, don't stick around like a sitting duck. Get far away from that wet mess and find some dry land. It's like when you're at the beach and you don't want to get sand in your shorts, except in this case it's arrows in your back.

4. Don't be a fool and try to attack an enemy army in the middle of a river crossing. Wait till at least half of them are across before you give 'em a piece of your mind.

    If you're trying to defend against an invading force, it might be tempting to meet them head-on as they're crossing the river. But Sun Tzu advises against this, suggesting instead that you wait until half the enemy army has crossed before attacking. That way, you can catch them off-guard and potentially take them by surprise. It's like letting the first wave of tourists go through the museum exhibits before you sneak in behind them to avoid the crowds.

5. If you're itching for a fight, don't make it easy for the enemy by meeting them near a river crossing. Make 'em work for it.

    Sun Tzu cautions against engaging the enemy near a river crossing if you're feeling anxious to fight. He's basically saying, "Calm down, soldier, and wait for the right moment." Maybe do some yoga or meditation to ease your nerves before going into battle.

6. Park your boat higher up the river than the enemy and keep your face to the sun. Don't try to paddle upstream and fight 'em head-on. That's all you need to know for river battles.

    Sun Tzu's advice on river warfare seems pretty solid, but it's also kind of specific. I mean, how often do you find yourself in a boat facing an enemy on a river? Unless you're a pirate or a Viking, probably not very often. But if you do, at least you know what to do.

7. When crossing a salt marsh, move fast and don't look back. It's like getting through a boring family dinner.

    Crossing salt-marshes sounds like a nightmare, and I'm not sure how much good Sun Tzu's advice will do you. I mean, if you're in a hurry to cross a salt-marsh, you're probably already running for your life. But hey, at least you know that Sun Tzu would want you to hurry up.

8. If you gotta fight in a salt marsh, make sure you have water, grass, and a good tree to hide behind. Think of it like a picnic with your enemies.

    But if you do end up having to fight in a salt-marsh, make sure you have water and grass nearby and get your back to a clump of trees. Sun Tzu is all about making the best of a bad situation, and in this case, he's saying to use the environment to your advantage.

9. If you're in flat, boring country, make sure you have high ground on your right and back so you can see danger coming. It's like setting up your tent at a music festival.

    If you're in a flat, open area, Sun Tzu recommends taking up a position with rising ground to your right and behind you. That way, you'll have a better view of the enemy's movements and you'll be able to retreat to safety if things go wrong. It's like playing a game of chess and protecting your king with your pawns.

10. These are the four super cool branches of military knowledge that helped the Yellow Emperor crush four different rulers.

11. Everyone knows high ground is better than low ground, and sunny spots are better than shady ones, even armies.

    Well, duh! Who wants to be stuck in a dark and damp place, right? High ground is great for getting a better view of the battlefield, but let's not forget that it's also great for those Instagram-worthy pics. As for the sunny places, well, they're perfect for getting that summer glow and working on your tan while you're at war.

12. If you take good care of your troops and camp on solid ground, your army won't catch any diseases and that's basically a recipe for victory.

    This is just common sense, folks. If you take care of your troops and keep them healthy, they'll be better equipped to fight. Plus, nobody wants to be stuck in a tent with a bunch of sniffling, sneezing soldiers. Ain't nobody got time for that!

13. When you come across a hill or slope, always occupy the sunny side with the slope on your right. This way, you'll make your soldiers happy and use the natural features of the terrain to your advantage.

    So, basically, if you're gonna climb a hill or a bank, make sure it's the sunny side. And if you're really feeling fancy, make sure your slope is on your right rear. This way, you'll be able to take advantage of all the natural perks that come with being on high ground. And let's face it, there's nothing better than a little sunshine to boost your mood and your morale.

14. If a river you need to cross is swollen and frothy due to heavy rains, just wait it out. Trying to ford it would be a terrible idea.

>Translation: "Don't be an idiot and try to cross a raging river." This is just common sense, people! Water can be dangerous, and if you're trying to cross a river that looks like it's about to burst its banks, you're gonna have a bad time. So, be patient, wait it out, and save yourself from a soggy and miserable fate. You'd be surprised how many armies have tried to ford a swollen river and ended up swimming with the fishes.

15. Stay away from areas with steep cliffs, rushing torrents, deep gullies, dense thickets, bogs, and ravines. Avoid them like the plague.
Translation: "Stay away from dangerous places." Got it. And if you do happen to come across these dangerous places, let the enemy have them on their rear. Because nothing says "victory" like letting your enemy fall off a cliff.

16. Instead, lure your enemies towards those hazardous places and then trap them. Turn their advantage into their downfall.

>Basically, don't be the one to fall into the traps we just talked about. Instead, lure your enemy into them, and watch them stumble and fall. And if you're feeling extra sneaky, let your enemy think they

have the upper hand and then surprise them with a surprise attack. That's how you win at war, folks.

17. If there's any hilly country, ponds, basins, or woods near your camp, search them carefully for spies and ambushes. Those sneaky enemies like to hide in those spots.

If you're in the wilderness and you come across any hills, ponds, basins or woods with dense undergrowth, you gotta be careful, my dude. Those places are probably crawling with sneaky spies or people waiting to ambush you. It's like playing hide and seek, but with real stakes.

18. If the enemy is just sitting tight and not making a move, he's probably confident in his position.

When the enemy is chilling and not making any moves, it's like when you're playing chess with your friend who's a total pro and they're just waiting for you to make a mistake. They're confident in their position, and they're waiting for you to slip up so they can say "checkmate, sucker!"

19. But if he's trying to provoke you into a fight, he's probably feeling anxious and trying to get you to make the first move.

When the enemy starts provoking you and get you to make the first move, it's like that annoying person who's always trying to start drama. Don't fall for their tricks, just stay focused on your own goals and don't let them distract you.

20. If the enemy's camp is easy to access, he's probably setting a trap. Watch out for bait and switch tactics.

 If the enemy's camp is easily accessible, it's like they're leaving a trail of breadcrumbs leading you straight into their trap. Don't fall for it! It's a classic move to lure you in and then pounce when you least expect it.

21. If you see trees moving like they're in a dance competition, it means the enemy is coming. If you spot a bunch of screens in the grass, the enemy is just trying to make you paranoid like your ex.

22. If birds suddenly fly away like they just heard some tea, it's an ambush. If the animals look like they've seen a ghost, it means the enemy is about to attack.

 Sun Tzu's statement that the rising of birds in flight is a sign of an ambush, and startled beasts indicate a sudden attack is coming is still true today. It's like when your cat suddenly jumps up and runs away for no apparent reason, you know something's up and you need to be on high alert. So, pay attention to the signals around you, and always be ready to react quickly.

23. If you see a big dust cloud rising up like it's trying to touch the sky, chariots are coming. If the dust is low and spread out like a Kardashian's contour, infantry is on its way. If the dust is all over the place, it's just the enemy collecting wood for their campfire. If the dust is moving around like a bunch of ants, the enemy is setting up camp.

Sun Tzu knew the importance of reading the signs of war, even if those signs were just dust clouds. I mean, let's face it, in modern times, we've got drones, satellites, and advanced intelligence gathering techniques, but back then, you had to rely on dust clouds. If you see a high column of dust, it's time to get your battle-ready chariots out. If it's low and spread out, well, get your infantry in position. And if you see dust moving back and forth, it's either a dance party or an army setting up camp.

24. If the enemy starts talking nice like they're trying to make up, they're probably planning something sneaky. If they start yelling like they're auditioning for a role in a Tarantino movie, they're likely to retreat.

Ah, the art of psychological warfare. If the enemy starts acting all meek and mild, while beefing up their defenses, then it's time to be on high alert because they're probably gearing up for an attack. On the other hand, if they're shouting and charging forward like they're going to crush us, then we can breathe a sigh of relief because they're probably bluffing and getting ready to retreat. It's kind of like when your little sibling tries to act tough by flexing their muscles, but you know they're just trying to compensate for something.

25. If you see the light chariots taking up positions on the wings, the enemy is getting ready for a fight. Or maybe they're just trying to impress their date.

If we see the enemy's light chariots positioning themselves on the sides of the battlefield, then we know that they're preparing for the main event. It's like when you're at a concert and the opening acts finish up, and the stage crew starts bringing out all the big gear. You know it's about to get lit!

26. If the enemy proposes peace without a sworn covenant, they're probably trying to pull a fast one on you.

You know what they say, if it sounds too good to be true, it probably is. If the enemy is suddenly proposing a peace treaty, but they're not willing to put it in writing, then we know that they're probably up to something. It's like when your roommate promises to pay rent on time but refuses to sign a lease agreement. Not a good sign!

27. When the soldiers start running around like they're in a game of musical chairs, it means the sh*t's about to hit the fan.

If we see our soldiers running around and getting into formation, we know that it's time to buckle up because things are about to get serious. It's like when you're at work, and everyone's frantically trying to meet a deadline, and the boss is hovering over you, making sure everything's perfect. The stakes are high, and it's time to bring your A-game!

28. If some soldiers are coming towards you while others are running away, it's a trap. Or maybe they're just playing a friendly game of tag.

If some of the enemy soldiers are advancing towards us while others are retreating, then we know that it's a trap! It's like when you're playing a game of dodgeball, and some of the other team members pretend to retreat, luring you into a false sense of security before they launch an all-out attack. Sneaky sneaky!

29. If the soldiers are leaning on their spears looking like they need a nap, it means they're starving. Or maybe they're just waiting for the food truck to arrive.

It's easy to forget that even the most battle-hardened soldiers need fuel to keep fighting. This is like when you're at work and you haven't had lunch yet, and suddenly everything seems insurmountable. Moral of the story? Keep some snacks nearby, and don't be afraid to take a break if you need one.

30. If the water collectors start drinking before they fill up the canteens, the army is thirsty AF.

This one's all about being prepared. If the people in charge of getting the water start drinking it all up themselves, then there's not enough to go around. It's like when you're on a road trip, and the driver drinks all the water before anyone else can get a sip - not cool. Always pack extra water, folks!

31. If the enemy isn't taking advantage of an obvious opportunity, it's probably because their soldiers are more tired than a mom with three kids under five.

When your enemy is too tired to even go after the low-hanging fruit, you know they're pretty wiped out. Sun Tzu is saying that if the enemy is too worn out to even take advantage of a clear opportunity, then you've got the upper hand. It's like when you're playing basketball and the other team misses an easy layup - you know they're not at their best, so it's time to pounce.

32. When birds gather on a spot, it's like an empty dance floor at a party. When there's a lot of noise at night, it's like the sound of your mom coming home early while you're having a house party.

Sun Tzu was like the original bird-watcher! He knew that if a bunch of birds were hanging out in one area, it probably meant that there were no people around. And if there's a lot of noise at night, it's a sign that people are on edge and not feeling secure. It's like when you're camping and you hear rustling in the bushes - you know there might be something out there, so you better be prepared.

33. If there's drama in the camp, the general's like the unpopular kid in high school. If the flags are shifting around, it's like a rebellion brewing. If the officers are angry, it's like your boss being grumpy because they had a bad day.

This is all about morale and leadership. If there's chaos and disorder in the camp, it's a sign that the general isn't doing a great job of keeping things in line. And if the banners and flags are being moved around, it means that someone is trying to undermine the leadership.

It's like when you're in a group project and everyone is arguing - you know the leader needs to step in and take control.

34. When an army starts feeding their horses better than their soldiers and killing their cows for dinner, you know things are getting serious. When they don't even bother cooking their food, it's like ordering takeout before a marathon.

This one's pretty intense - it's all about the willingness to fight until the bitter end. If an army is killing their own cattle for food, it means they're not planning on going back home anytime soon. And if they're not even bothering to hang their pots over the fire, they're ready for a battle that could last a while. It's like when you're in a video game and you're down to your last sliver of health - you know you're in trouble, but you're not going down without a fight.

35. When soldiers start whispering and gossiping, it's like a group chat without the admin. When they're speaking in hushed tones, it's like when you're trying to talk to your friend in class without the teacher noticing.

This is all about detecting dissent within the ranks. If you see people whispering and talking in hushed tones, it means that they're not happy with the way things are going. It's like when you're at a party and everyone is whispering about how much they hate the music - you know there's trouble brewing. The key is to address the issues before they turn into something bigger.

36. If the enemy starts giving out too many rewards, it's like they're trying to bribe you with candy. If they're punishing their soldiers too much, it's like they're a parent who just found out their kid got a bad grade.

So, when your enemy starts to hand out participation trophies like candy, it's a pretty good sign that they're running low on morale and resources. And on the other hand, if they start dishing out punishment left and right, then they're probably in a state of desperate distress. It's like they're saying, "Hey, we're out of ideas, so let's just beat up our own soldiers until something good happens!"

37. When you start trash-talking but then get scared, it's like a rapper who can't handle a rap battle.

It's like talking a big game but then immediately chickening out. That's just embarrassing. It's like getting into a bar fight and yelling, "You want a piece of me?!" and then turning around and running away when the other guy actually takes you up on the offer.

38. If the enemy sends envoys with compliments, it's like a guy sending flowers after a breakup.

Ah, compliments. The ultimate passive-aggressive move. When your enemy starts sending envoys with honeyed words and pleasantries, it's a sure sign that they're looking for a way to take a breather. It's like saying, "We could keep fighting, but let's be real, we're both getting tired. Can we just call a timeout for a bit?"

39. If the enemy is angry and just stands there, it's like a staring contest that no one wants to break.

    If your enemy is just standing there, staring you down, and not making a move, it's time to get worried. It's like they're saying, "We're not attacking, but we're definitely not leaving either. We're just going to stand here and make you really uncomfortable until you slip up."

40. If the enemy is the same size as your army, it's like two people standing in front of each other with their arms crossed. The key is to stay focused and wait for reinforcements like getting your squad to back you up.

    Quantity isn't everything. You can still win a battle even if you're outnumbered - you just need to be smart about your tactics and use your resources wisely. And if all else fails, call for backup.

41. If you don't take your opponent seriously, you're like a cat playing with a mouse. Eventually, they'll catch you off guard.

    Arrogance will get you nowhere in war. If you think you're invincible and don't bother to plan ahead, you're just asking to get taken down. It's like walking into a test without studying and thinking you'll just wing it. Sure, you might get lucky, but more likely than not, you're going to fail miserably.

42. If you punish soldiers too early, it's like a boss yelling at an intern on their first day. If you don't punish them at all, it's like letting your dog get away with everything.

Ah yes, the classic "tough love" approach. You know what they say, "the army runs on fear and caffeine". But seriously, this quote highlights the importance of building trust and loyalty with soldiers before laying down the law. Punishing them right off the bat is a surefire way to make them resentful and rebellious. It's like trying to discipline a toddler who's not attached to you yet - good luck with that!

43. You need to treat soldiers with kindness but also discipline them, like a strict but loving parent. That's the way to win.

"Humanity" and "iron discipline" - two things that don't exactly go together like peanut butter and jelly. But Sun Tzu is basically saying that soldiers need to be treated with respect and compassion, but also kept in line with a firm hand. It's a delicate balance, kind of like being a parent to a teenager. You want to be cool and understanding, but also make sure they don't burn the house down.

44. If you don't enforce commands during training, your army will be like a bunch of kids on a field trip. But if you do, they'll be like a well-oiled machine.

This speaks to the importance of consistency and follow-through when it comes to training soldiers. If you let them get away with breaking the rules once, they'll be more likely to do it again. Of course, there's a difference between enforcing the rules and being overly harsh or punitive.

45. If a general has faith in their soldiers and gives clear orders, it's like a coach who trusts their team to win the game.

Sun Tzu is emphasizing the importance of trust and respect between a general and their soldiers. If a general shows confidence in their troops, it can boost morale and motivate them to perform at their best. But, of course, orders still need to be followed for the sake of the mission and the safety of everyone involved. This still holds true today, even outside of military contexts. It's important for leaders to show faith in their team members and empower them to take ownership of their work, while also maintaining clear expectations and holding everyone accountable. Mutual trust and respect are key ingredients for any successful team, whether in the workplace, sports, or any other setting.

X. Terrain

1. Yo, Sun Tzu here. Check it, there's six types of terrain:

    (1) Easy access,

    (2) Tricky AF,

    (3) Play it cool,

    (4) Tight squeezes,

    (5) Scary heights, and

    (6) Far AF from the enemy.

Sun Tzu was a master strategist, and he knew that understanding the lay of the land was crucial for military success. In this quote, he outlines six types of terrain and their strategic implications. " Easy access " is easy to move through, while " Tricky

AF " is more difficult and slows down progress. " Play it cool " allows for stalling and delaying tactics, while " Tight squeezes " create chokepoints and make it easier to defend against attackers. " Scary heights " give a tactical advantage in terms of visibility and ambush points, while " Far AF from the enemy " can be used to avoid direct conflict and wear down the enemy over time.

This can still be useful today, even outside of military contexts. Understanding the terrain of a particular situation or problem can help us make more informed decisions and come up with better strategies. Whether it's navigating a physical landscape or a business environment, knowing the lay of the land is key to success.

2. If both you and your enemy can easily move around on the ground, it's Easy access.

3. When you're on accessible ground, you gotta hustle to nab the high spots and make sure your supplies are on lock. That way, you'll have the upper hand in a fight.

4. Tricky AF ground can be bailed on, but it's a real pain to reclaim. If the enemy's not ready, you can jump 'em. But if they're prepared and you can't get back, you're screwed.

5. Now, if you happen to find yourself on some Tricky AF ground and the enemy ain't ready for your swag, then you can slide in and take them out like a boss. But if they're ready for your move and you don't

come out on top, well, let's just say you ain't coming back from that one.

6. Play it cool ground means neither side wants to make the first move. Just chill and wait for the right moment to strike.

 This term means that there is a strategic advantage in waiting and not making the first move, especially when both sides are at a stalemate. In simpler terms, it means that sometimes it's better to do nothing and let the other side make a move first.

7. If you're in this position and the enemy is dangling a juicy carrot in front of you, don't take the bait and charge forward like a rabid bunny. Instead, fall back and lead the enemy into your trap like a sneaky fox. When they take the bait and come out to play, pounce on them like a hungry lion and give them a taste of your ferocity.

8. If you can snag a Tight squeezes ground before your enemy, fortify that sh*t and wait for them to come to you.

 When it comes to Tight squeezes ground, it's like trying to get into a packed club on a Saturday night. If you can get in there first, make sure you have a strong crew with you and wait for the party to come to you.

9. If the enemy's already taken a Tight squeezes ground, only go after 'em if they're weakly guarded. Otherwise, don't even bother.

But if you get there and find out your ex has already gotten in with their new fling, don't go charging in unless you know their crew is weak. Otherwise, you're just asking for a beatdown.

10. When it comes to those Scary heights, if you get there first, make sure to snag the sunny and elevated spots and wait for your enemy to catch up. But if they beat you to it, don't be a fool and follow them, retreat and try to lure them away like a game of tag.

Who doesn't love a good view from the top? If you're lucky enough to snag a scary height before the enemy, make sure to grab the best spot with the most sun and wait for them to come up to you. It's like being the cool kid who gets the best seat on the bus ride to the field trip. Just don't get too cocky up there, because the enemy might have a few tricks up their sleeve.

11. If you're chillin' far away from your enemy and your armies seem pretty evenly matched, it's gonna be tough to get them to fight. It's like trying to get two stubborn toddlers to share a toy. Not worth it, my dude.

If you and your enemies are separated by a great distance and your armies are evenly matched, it may not be wise to try and provoke a battle. This is because if the enemy is smart, they won't take the bait and you'll just be wasting your time and resources trying to draw them out.

Instead, you might want to consider other strategies like trying to weaken their army by cutting off their supply lines, or launching surprise attacks on their weak points. It's all about finding the right balance between being patient and aggressive.

    In my opinion this advice is still relevant today, especially in situations where both sides are equally matched. It's important to weigh the potential risks and benefits of different strategies before making a move. Sometimes it's better to wait and bide your time than to rush into a battle that you might not win.

12. These are the six things you gotta know about Earth, my general. Don't forget it, or you'll be looking like a fool on the battlefield.

13. So, like, an army can get totally screwed over by six things that have nothing to do with Mother Nature, but everything to do with the general. They are:
    (1) Running away like a scaredy-cat;
    (2) refusing to listen to orders;
    (3) collapsing like a house of cards;
    (4) getting wrecked like a car crash;
    (5) becoming a hot mess of disorganization;
    (6) running away in complete and utter chaos.

    These six things that can screw up an army's chances of victory are all related to the leadership and organization of the army. Running away, refusing to listen to orders, collapsing, getting wrecked, becoming disorganized, and running away in chaos are all signs of poor leadership, lack of discipline, and inadequate training.

Sun Tzu's advice is clear: to win a battle, a general must be a strong leader who can inspire confidence in his soldiers, keep them organized and disciplined, and make quick and effective decisions. He also emphasizes the importance of knowing one's own strengths and weaknesses, as well as those of the enemy, and adapting one's strategy accordingly.

In a modern context, these principles are still relevant in many areas of life, from business to sports to personal relationships. A good leader must be able to inspire and motivate their team, while also being able to adapt to changing circumstances and make effective decisions. Ultimately, success depends not just on talent or resources, but also on the quality of leadership and organization.

14. Look, if you pit a tiny force against a huge one, unless some serious divine intervention goes down, the little guys are gonna run away like Usain Bolt.

This point is pretty straightforward - if one army is much smaller than the other, they're likely to flee rather than face certain defeat. It's not exactly rocket science, but it's important to remember that numbers do matter in warfare. I mean, this is just common sense. It's like trying to take down a raid boss in a video game when you're severely under-leveled. It's not gonna end well.

15. When the grunts are too strong and their bosses are too weak, that's a recipe for insubordination. When the bosses are too strong and the grunts are too weak, it's like a house of cards waiting to fall.

This point highlights the delicate balance of power between officers and soldiers. If the officers are too weak and the soldiers are too strong, the soldiers might start to ignore orders and do their own thing. Conversely, if the officers are too strong and the soldiers are too weak, the soldiers might not be able to handle the pressure and collapse under it. This is like a classic power dynamic issue. It's important for leaders to strike a balance between maintaining authority and giving their subordinates enough autonomy to do their jobs effectively.

16. When the higher-ups are all ticked off and start fighting the enemy on their own, without waiting for orders, that's just pure stupidity. It's like trying to play a team sport without a coach.

In modern times, we might call this a case of "office politics gone wrong." When the higher-ups are more interested in their own egos and grudges than the well-being of the army, disaster is sure to follow. It's like a bunch of coworkers getting into a shouting match and throwing staplers at each other instead of doing their jobs.

17. When the general is a total pushover, and nobody knows what the heck is going on, and everybody's just winging it, it's a complete and utter disaster.

This is a classic case of "failure to communicate." When everyone is on a different page and no one is taking charge, things quickly fall apart. It's like trying to plan a party with a group of indecisive friends who can't agree on anything and leave everything until the last minute. So, yeah, don't be a weakling, be a boss. Give clear orders, assign specific duties, and make sure your troops are lined up like they're going to a VIP club. Otherwise, your army is gonna turn into a chaotic mess.

18. When a general sends a weak army to fight a stronger one without any backup plan, it's like bringing a knife to a gunfight. The result? Epic fail.
This is like going into a fight without knowing who you're up against, and not putting your best fighters at the front. It's a recipe for disaster, and the same goes for a military campaign. If the general can't properly assess the enemy's strength and doesn't put the best soldiers in the most important positions, they're gonna get crushed.

19. These are six surefire ways to lose a battle: underestimate your enemy, overestimate yourself, ignore the terrain, forget to strategize, neglect your soldiers, and eat a burrito right before the fight.

Basically, these are the things that a general needs to avoid if they want to be successful. It's like a checklist of what not to do, and if a general can avoid these six things, they'll have a much better chance of victory.

20. The terrain is your bestie, but a great leader knows how to size up the enemy, control their own troops, and expertly navigate any obstacles. That's the real test of being a boss general.

The natural formation of the country can be your ally, just like your friends who can help you win a game of Fortnite. But if you want to be a great general, you gotta be able to read the battlefield like a pro gamer reads a game. You gotta know where the loot is, where the enemies are, and how to use your resources wisely.

21. If you got the skills and use 'em in battle, you'll be the one to win. But if you don't have a clue and don't bother practicing, you'll end up losing like a total fool.

Knowing is half the battle, as they say. But actually putting that knowledge into practice is what separates the winners from the losers. It's like studying for a test but then not bothering to show up on exam day. If you don't apply what you've learned, you're bound to fail. And in war, failure can mean death or defeat. So, study up and put your knowledge to work.

22. If you're gonna win, go for it, even if your boss says no. But if you're gonna lose, don't even bother, even if your boss is like, 'Come on, man, do it for me!'

This principle sounds a bit rebellious, but it makes sense. Sometimes, rulers or leaders may have their own agendas and may not always make the best decisions for their country or army. If a general knows that fighting will lead to victory, it's their duty to do what's best for their soldiers and their nation, even if it means going against orders. But on the other hand, if fighting is not going to result in victory, then it's better to avoid unnecessary bloodshed, even if the ruler demands it. In other words, don't be a yes-man and think for yourself.

In all seriousness, this passage highlights the importance of strategic decision-making in warfare. It's not just about blindly following orders or being aggressive at all costs. A great general must assess the situation and make the best decision for their country, even if it means going against their ruler's wishes. On the other hand, if the odds are against them, it's not worth sacrificing lives and resources for a losing battle, no matter how much the ruler wants it.

23. The greatest generals aren't the ones who seek fame or glory. They're the ones who fight for their country and their people, no matter what. Plus, they look really cool in those military uniforms.

This is all about having the right motivation and mindset. A great general should not be motivated by personal gain or glory, but by a desire to protect their country and serve their leader. It's like being a selfless hero who puts the needs of others before their own. And a great general should be able to retreat strategically without fearing disgrace or criticism. It's not always about winning every battle, but about the bigger picture and long-term goals. So, be selfless, strategic, and always keep the bigger picture in mind.

24. Treat your soldiers like your own children, and they'll follow you to the ends of the earth. But if you treat them like annoying little siblings, they'll probably just ditch you and go play video games.

This one is all about leadership and how you treat your soldiers. Sun Tzu is saying that if you treat your soldiers like your own children, with love and care, they will be loyal to you and follow you anywhere. But if you're a pushover who can't enforce your commands, then your soldiers will act like spoiled children, and nobody wants that. So, the lesson here is to be a cool parent, but also one who means business.

25. If you're a weak leader who can't control your troops, then you're basically screwed. Your soldiers will be like a bunch of toddlers on a sugar high, and they'll do whatever they want.

Okay, so this is the flip side of the last advice. If you're too soft on your soldiers and can't get them to listen to you, then they're basically useless. It's like trying to wrangle a group of unruly toddlers - if you can't establish some sort of authority, they'll just run rampant and get nothing done. So, as a leader, it's important to find that balance between being kind and understanding, but also being able to assert your authority when necessary.

26. It's not enough to just know that your troops are ready for battle. You also have to know whether your enemy is actually vulnerable. Otherwise, you're just wasting your time.

It's not enough to just have your own troops ready for battle - you also need to be aware of the enemy's weaknesses and vulnerabilities. If you charge into battle without knowing if the enemy is actually vulnerable, you're only halfway towards victory. It's like playing a game of chess - you need to be aware of your opponent's moves and anticipate their next move in order to win.

27. You might think you're ready to take on the enemy, but if your own soldiers are feeling sick or hungover or just plain lazy, you're not gonna

get very far. So make sure everyone is at their best before charging into battle.

This advice is the opposite of the previous one - it's saying that even if you know that the enemy is vulnerable, you can't win if your own troops aren't ready for battle. It's like having a game plan but not having the players to execute it. So, as a leader, it's important to not only assess the enemy's weaknesses, but also make sure your own troops are in fighting condition before charging into battle.

28. Even if your soldiers are pumped up and ready to fight, the terrain can make all the difference. You might have the best soldiers in the world, but if you're fighting on a steep hill covered in mud, you're gonna have a bad time.

Sun Tzu here reminds us that it's not enough to simply know that the enemy is vulnerable and that our own soldiers are ready to attack - we also need to consider the terrain we're fighting on. It's like trying to play a game of dodgeball in a room full of obstacles - it doesn't matter how good your aim is or how fast you can throw if you keep tripping over chairs and tables. As a modern analogy, it's like trying to parkour through a city without taking into account the height of buildings or the slipperiness of the pavement. So, we must always be aware of the terrain we're fighting on and how it might affect our tactics.

29. A great general never gets lost or confused. They know where they're going, and they always have a plan. Plus, they probably have a really good GPS.

Sun Tzu emphasizes the importance of staying in motion and being decisive once we've made a plan. It's like starting a road trip - once you hit the highway, you have a destination in mind and you keep moving towards it. You don't constantly second-guess yourself and turn around every time you see a new sign or exit ramp. The same goes for military campaigns - once you've broken camp and set your sights on the enemy, you don't hesitate or lose your way.

30. If you really want to win a battle, you need to know everything there is to know about your enemy and your surroundings. Think of it like playing Call of Duty, but in real life.

Sun Tzu concludes by summing up his key advice: know yourself, know your enemy, know heaven, and know earth. In other words, be aware of your own strengths and weaknesses, study your opponent's strengths and weaknesses, consider the larger context and forces at play (heaven), and understand the terrain you're fighting on (earth). It's like playing a game of chess - you need to understand the capabilities of each piece, the moves your opponent might make, the overall strategy you're pursuing, and the layout of the board. And just like in chess, the more you understand these factors, the more likely you are to win the game.

XI. The Nine Situations

1.Sun Tzu, the OG war strategist, said there are nine types of ground: Dispersive, facile, contentious, open, intersecting highways, serious, difficult, hemmed-in, and desperate. Kind of like a choose-your-own-adventure book, but with way more bloodshed.

2. When a chieftain is defending his own turf, it's that Dispersive ground, you feel me?

3. But when he's in enemy territory, but not too far in, that's what we call Facile ground.

4. If both sides can gain a big advantage from controlling a certain area, then you're dealing with some Contentious ground.

5. Open ground is when both armies can move around pretty freely, like a game of chess with no pawns in the way.

6. If a piece of land connects three different states, and whoever gets there first gets the upper hand, that's some real Game of Thrones level Intersecting Highways ground.

7. When an army is deep in enemy territory, surrounded by fortified cities, that's some Serious ground. No jokes, no laughs, just pure business.

8. If you're dealing with mountains, forests, swamps, or anything that's hard to get through, that's Difficult ground. You might as well be playing a game of hide and seek blindfolded.

9. Picture this: you're at a party and you accidentally find yourself in a cramped corner where you can barely move. Now imagine your arch-nemesis shows up with a couple of their friends. You're screwed, right? That's hemmed in ground, my friend. It's like being stuck in a narrow alley with a gang of angry cats. You want to avoid it at all costs in battle because it's basically a death trap for your troops.

10. And last but not least, when you're totally trapped with no way out, you're on that Desperate ground. Might as well start saying your prayers now.

11. The rules are simple: don't fight on dispersive ground, don't stop on facile ground, and don't attack on contentious ground.

12. On open ground, don't try to block the enemy's path. On intersecting highways ground, team up with your allies for the ultimate power play.

This is like saying, "Don't be a roadblock on a busy street, but if you're at a crossroads, team up with your squad." In other words, don't get in the way of progress, but if there's an opportunity to work together, take it.

13. In serious ground, loot everything you can. In difficult ground, just keep on marching.

"When the going gets tough, the tough get looting." No, but seriously, in a serious battle, it's important to take advantage of any opportunities for loot and resources. On difficult terrain, just keep pushing forward without stopping.

14. If you're stuck in hemmed-in ground, you better start coming up with some sneaky tactics. And if you're on desperate ground, well, it's time to start swinging.

When you're in a tight spot, use your brain and come up with clever strategies to outmaneuver your opponent. When things get desperate, it's time to fight with everything you've got.

15. Those old-school leaders knew how to really mess with the enemy. They'd split their forces up and keep them from working together - kind of like causing a massive fight in Among Us.

In any competition, it's important to try and disrupt your opponent's strategy and prevent them from working together. By dividing and conquering, you can gain an advantage and come out on top.

16. They'd also keep the enemy in chaos and disarray, because a confused enemy is a weak enemy.

By keeping the enemy in disarray, the skilled leaders were able to gain the upper hand and secure their victories. They were experts at exploiting weaknesses and turning them into opportunities.

17. They knew when to make their move and when to hold back, kind of like timing your jump in a game of Mario.

This sounds like a pretty reasonable approach, doesn't it? I mean, why charge forward into battle if it's not going to benefit you in some way? This principle is a good one to follow, but with some caution. You don't want to be so focused on your own advantage that you neglect the needs and interests of others, whether they be your allies or the people you're fighting against. Ultimately, success in war is not just about winning battles, but also about building alliances and creating long-term stability.

18. And if you're wondering how to deal with a massive enemy army, just take something they really love and hold it hostage. You'll have them eating out of the palm of your hand.

Ah, the classic "hit 'em where it hurts" strategy. It's true that if you can take away something your enemy values, they'll be more likely to listen to your demands. It's like if someone steals your phone – you're going to be more willing to do what they say if they promise to give it back!

19. The key to victory? Speed. Catch your enemy off-guard, sneak up on them from unexpected angles, and hit them where it hurts.

This principle emphasizes the importance of speed and surprise in war. By moving quickly and unpredictably, you can catch your opponent off-guard and take advantage of their weaknesses before they have a chance to react. This is easier said than done. In practice, it can be very difficult to move quickly and quietly through hostile territory, and even harder to identify unguarded spots or exploit your opponent's unreadiness without putting yourself in danger. However, if you can pull it off, the rewards can be huge.

20. And if you're invading a new territory, just remember - the further you go, the stronger your team will be. And always raid the good farming spots for some sweet, sweet supplies.

Here it is all about the logistics of invading and occupying foreign territory. It suggests that the deeper you go into enemy territory, the more your troops will bond and become resistant to counter-attacks. It also emphasizes the importance of securing a reliable food source in order to sustain your forces.

21. Yo troops, don't forget to hit up them lush farming spots for some fresh grub! Gotta keep those bellies full if we wanna win this war. No more stale MREs, let's get some farm-to-table action going on.
Translation: Don't let your soldiers starve, steal from the farmers instead.

22. Take a page out of my book and listen up, war strategists! You gotta treat your troops right, or they'll be as useless as a screen door on a submarine. Don't push them too hard, save your energy, and come up with crazy plans that'll blow the enemy's mind.

You don't want your soldiers to be burnt out and exhausted before the big battle. So, as a leader, it's important to prioritize their well-being and make sure they're not being overworked. Also, you need to stay focused and save your energy for the right moment. This is like being the captain of a sports team and making sure your players are well-rested and ready for the big game. And, of course, you need to keep things interesting with some unpredictable plays and strategies.

23. Corner your soldiers so they have no way out, and watch them choose death before defeat. When they're fearless, there's no limit to what they can do. Both officers and grunts will give it their all.

    This is some pretty hardcore advice. The idea here is that if you back your soldiers into a corner where they have no way out, they'll fight harder and more fiercely than ever before. It's like the classic "fight or flight" response. If your soldiers feel like they have no choice but to fight, they'll be more motivated to do their best. But this is definitely not a strategy for the faint of heart.

24. When your soldiers are up against the wall, they lose all sense of fear. If there's no place to run, they'll stand tall. If they're deep in enemy territory, they'll fight like there's no tomorrow. They'll go all-out when they have nothing left to lose.

    This is another way of saying that when people are pushed to their limits, they can surprise themselves with what they're capable of. When there's nowhere to run and no easy way out, soldiers will be more likely to stand their ground and fight with all they've got. It's like being in a tough situation where you have no choice but to persevere. And sometimes, that's when you discover what you're really made of.

25. Keep your troops alert at all times, and they'll obey you without question. When there are no rules, they'll stay true to your cause. You can trust them with your life without even giving orders.

This is the ultimate goal of any leader - to have a group of soldiers who are so loyal and committed that they don't need to be told what to do. They're always on the lookout for ways to help, they'll do anything you ask of them, and they'll never let you down. It's like having a group of superpowered sidekicks who are always ready to jump into action at a moment's notice. But, of course, getting to this level of trust and loyalty takes time and effort.

26. Enough with the superstitions and bad omens. Don't fear anything, not even death itself, and you'll never face a calamity.

This piece of advice may sound strange to us in the modern world where superstition and belief in omens are not taken very seriously. However, in Sun Tzu's time, these beliefs were prevalent and could have a significant impact on the morale of soldiers. By advising to prohibit taking omens and getting rid of superstitious doubts, Sun Tzu was essentially saying that soldiers should focus on what they can control and not worry about things outside of their control. This is a timeless lesson that can still be applied today in any situation where we are tempted to worry about things we cannot change.

27. Your soldiers aren't poor because they don't want riches, and they don't live short lives because they hate longevity. Don't make them

rich, but give them what they need. Don't make them live forever, but let them make the most of their time.

In this passage, Sun Tzu is emphasizing the importance of understanding the motivations and needs of soldiers. He suggests that soldiers are not necessarily disinterested in wealth or long life, but rather that these things may not be a top priority when compared to the demands of military service.

When soldiers are burdened with too much money or are overly focused on personal wealth, it can distract them from their duties and compromise their effectiveness on the battlefield. Similarly, if soldiers are too preoccupied with their own well-being, it can make them more risk-averse and less willing to take the necessary risks in combat.

Sun Tzu is suggesting that soldiers must be motivated by a sense of duty and loyalty to their cause, rather than by personal gain. By emphasizing the importance of this kind of selflessness, Sun Tzu is underscoring the importance of leadership that inspires soldiers to put the needs of the group ahead of their own individual desires. This passage speaks to a fundamental truth about human motivation: people are willing to sacrifice personal comfort and safety when they believe in a cause that is greater than themselves. Sun Tzu's advice to leaders is to cultivate this sense of purpose in their soldiers, so that they will be motivated to fight with courage and determination even in the face of great adversity.

28. Your troops may cry and weep when they're first ordered to battle, but when they're cornered, they'll fight like heroes. They'll be fearless and unstoppable, like warriors from Chu or Kuei.

Sun Tzu understood that fear and anxiety are natural emotions that soldiers may experience before going into battle. However, he believed that once soldiers are faced with the reality of combat, their training and instincts will kick in, and they will rise to the occasion. This is a timeless lesson that can be applied to any situation where we may feel afraid or uncertain. We should trust in our abilities and training, and have confidence that we can handle whatever challenges come our way.

29. If you want to be a top-notch strategist, learn from the shuai-jan. It's a snake from the Chung mountains that'll attack you no matter where you hit it. But you can make your army imitate it, and they'll be invincible.

Sun Tzu often used analogies to explain his points, and the shuai-jan snake is a great example of his teaching method. By likening a skilled tactician to the shuai-jan, Sun Tzu was saying that a tactician should be unpredictable and have the ability to attack from unexpected angles. The shuai-jan snake is known for its ability to attack from both ends, and a skilled tactician should be able to do the same. This is a lesson that can be applied not only to warfare but to any situation where one needs to be strategic and think outside the box.

30. Even sworn enemies can put their differences aside when they're in the same boat. Literally. If the men of Wu and Yueh are caught in a storm while crossing a river together, they'll help each other out like a left hand helping a right.

Wow, that's actually kind of heartwarming. Maybe we could all learn a thing or two from the men of Wu and Yueh. After all, we're all in the same boat (metaphorically speaking). Maybe instead of fighting each other, we should work together to weather life's storms. Or at least not push each other overboard. Even enemies can put their differences aside and work together when faced with a common enemy. It's like when your rival team comes to help you carry your fallen teammate off the field, even though you were just trying to crush each other a minute ago. It's a heartwarming reminder that we're all human, and sometimes we need each other to survive.

31. You can't just rely on tying up horses and burying chariot wheels in the dirt, we need some actual strategy here people!

This statement suggests that military leaders must not rely solely on defensive measures such as tethering horses and burying chariot wheels, but must also have a more strategic and proactive approach to warfare. In modern terms, it would be like saying that relying only on traditional military tactics such as tanks and planes without adapting to new technologies and strategies is not enough. It's important to stay ahead of the game and constantly adapt to new challenges.

32. Listen up soldiers, our motto is 'one standard of courage for all'...unless you're the general, then you can have a little extra.

This statement suggests that a military leader should set a standard of courage that all soldiers must meet in order to be effective. This is important for creating a cohesive and strong army that can work together towards a common goal. In modern terms, it's like setting a high standard for teamwork and collaboration within an organization to ensure that everyone is on the same page and working towards a shared goal.

33. The key to success is knowing how to use your strengths and weaknesses to your advantage, like posting your sick gains on social media and pretending you're not addicted to TikTok.

Military leaders must understand how to use their resources, both strong and weak, to their best advantage. This includes understanding the terrain and how to position troops strategically to gain the upper hand. In modern terms, it's like saying that success in any endeavor requires a thorough understanding of one's resources and how to leverage them effectively.

34. A good general leads his troops like he's babysitting a single child, except this child has swords and could kill you if you mess up.

A skillful general must have a deep understanding of each soldier under his command and lead them individually towards a common goal. In modern terms, it's like saying that effective leadership requires a personalized approach that takes into account the unique strengths and weaknesses of each team member.

35. As a general, it's important to be quiet like a mouse and just like your ex's social media photos - no one needs to know what you're up to.

In modern times, we might say that a good leader should be like a ninja: stealthy, strategic, and always one step ahead. Being quiet and keeping secrets can be powerful tools to maintain control and order. But at the same time, a leader must also be upright and just, to gain the trust and respect of their followers. You can't lead effectively if your own people don't believe in you.

36. You gotta keep your troops on their toes by confusing them with fake news and alternative facts, just like a certain former president we all know.

Sun Tzu advises that a general must be able to deceive his own officers and soldiers with false reports and appearances in order to keep them in ignorance. This means that the general should not reveal his true intentions or strategies to his own troops in order to prevent leaks of information to the enemy.

Deception has been used throughout history as a tactic in warfare, from the Trojan Horse to modern-day espionage. In modern warfare, military forces use sophisticated technology and techniques to deceive the enemy, such as creating false targets or using electronic jamming to disrupt enemy communications.

In my personal opinion, while deception can be a useful tactic in warfare, it should not be relied upon too heavily. If a general relies too much on deception, it can create mistrust and suspicion among their own troops, and may even lead to friendly fire incidents. A general should balance the use of deception with open and honest communication with their own soldiers and officers.

37. If the enemy thinks they know what you're gonna do next, you gotta switch things up like you're a Netflix algorithm trying to keep us all entertained.

Flexibility and adaptability are crucial traits for any leader, especially in times of war. Being able to change plans on the fly and keep the enemy guessing can give you a significant advantage.

38. When it's time to make a move, the general should act like a sneaky cat burglar who climbs up a building and then breaks all the fire escapes so no one can follow.

Sometimes, taking a bold and risky move can pay off big time. But it's important to weigh the risks and benefits carefully before making any major decisions. You don't want to put your team in unnecessary danger just for the sake of a surprise attack. And if you do decide to go for it, make sure you have a solid plan and backup options in case things go wrong.

39. Burn those boats and smash those pots, because we're in this for the long haul and there's no turning back now. Just like when you delete your ex's number after a bad breakup.

Well, that escalated quickly. Burning boats and breaking cooking pots? Sounds like a party gone wrong. But I guess this is war, not a picnic. A good general needs to keep their troops on their toes, never let them get too comfortable. Drive them this way and that, keep them guessing. They might not know where they're going, but hey, that's half the fun, right? And who needs boats and cooking pots anyway? We're soldiers, not chefs!

Sun Tzu is describing a strategy that involves a leader cutting off all means of retreat and committing to a path of action without any possibility of turning back. This is illustrated by the metaphor of burning boats and breaking cooking pots, which means that the leader eliminates any possibility of retreating or reversing course, forcing the soldiers to move forward with him. The leader must keep his soldiers in the dark, unable to predict his next move or goal.

Sun Tzu is emphasizing the importance of commitment and boldness in leadership. If a leader hesitates or leaves an escape route, his soldiers may lose faith in his ability to lead and may not follow him with the same conviction. By taking away the possibility of retreat, the leader forces his soldiers to fight with all their might and overcome any obstacles in their way.

While this strategy may work in some situations, it is also risky and can lead to disastrous consequences if the leader misjudges the situation or underestimates the enemy. A leader must balance the need for boldness and commitment with strategic thinking and flexibility. Cutting off all retreat options may lead to a decisive victory, but it also leaves no room for error or escape if the situation turns against the leader.

40. The general's main job is to round up the troops and put them in harm's way. You know, like a really intense game of dodgeball.
Ah, the good old business of putting your troops in danger. That's what a general is for, right?

In other words, the general's job is not just to lead his army into battle, but also to gather and organize his troops in a way that puts them at risk. This may seem counterintuitive, but it's actually a key strategy for success in warfare.

From a modern perspective, this could be seen as the general's responsibility to take calculated risks and make bold decisions. It's not just about having the biggest army or the best weapons, but also about being strategic and proactive in putting your troops in a position to win.
Of course, this doesn't mean needlessly putting your soldiers in harm's way. Rather, it means carefully planning and executing maneuvers that will give your army the best chance of success, even if it involves some level of risk.

41. You gotta study the terrain, the tactics, and human nature if you wanna win this war. Also, maybe take a few online courses while you're at it.

    Strategy, tactics, and human nature - these are the things a general must understand if they want to be successful. It's not just about brute force and strength. You have to be able to read your opponent, know the lay of the land, and understand how people will react in different situations.

42. If you're gonna invade, you better commit to it like a college student with a 3am Taco Bell order - deep penetration or nothing at all.

    Invading hostile territory is like going into someone's house uninvited. If you just stick around near the door, you're likely to get kicked out quickly. But if you push deeper into the house and start rearranging the furniture, you're more likely to get the people inside to band together and fight you off. As a general, you need to know how far to push into enemy territory without spreading your troops too thin.

43. Yo, when you take your squad into new territory, that's some critical ground. And if there are roads everywhere, it's like you're in a maze, yo.

    Leaving your own country to invade another is a big deal. You're not just fighting on unfamiliar territory, you're also dealing with a different culture and possibly a different language. When you're on neighborhood territory, you're in a delicate position because you don't want to upset the people around you too much. And if there are highways or other means of communication on all sides, you're basically fighting in a fishbowl where everyone can see what you're doing.

44. If you go deep into enemy territory, it's no joke, serious ground. But if you only go a little way, it's like a piece of cake, easy ground.

Going deep into enemy territory is like diving into the deep end of the pool. It's serious business, and you need to know what you're doing. But if you're just splashing around in the shallow end, it's not that big of a deal. As a general, you need to decide how far you're willing to go into enemy territory and what your objectives are. Sometimes it's better to go deep and strike at the enemy's heart, and sometimes it's better to just poke around and harass them.

45. If the enemy's got you surrounded and there's no escape, you're on some hemmed-in ground. And if there's no place to hide, you're on some desperate ground, my friend.

46. So, if you're on facile ground, make sure everyone in your army is tight. And if you're on hemmed-in ground, make sure your back-up's coming in hot.

47. On contentious ground, move fast and keep your head up, yo.

48. On open ground, keep your defenses strong, don't let anyone slip through. And on some intersecting highways ground, make sure your alliances are solid.

49. On some serious ground, make sure your supplies are on point, don't let your squad go hungry. And on tough ground, don't stop pushing forward.

50. If you're on trapped ground, make sure there's no way out. And if you're on some desperate ground, let your squad know it's all or nothing.

51. 'Cause soldiers will fight like hell when they're cornered and in danger, and follow orders when it counts.

    This passage highlights the importance of understanding the psychology of soldiers in battle. It's important for a general to know that soldiers are more likely to fight harder and follow orders when they are in danger or surrounded. However, this doesn't mean a general should put their soldiers in unnecessary danger. A good general should inspire their soldiers to fight with bravery and discipline.

52. You can't team up with other homies unless you know their game. And you can't lead a squad through rough terrain unless you know the land like the back of your hand. And if you don't know the land, get yourself a guide, yo.

It's essential to have local guides who know the lay of the land and can help avoid dangerous traps and ambushes. It's also crucial to gather intelligence about the enemy's plans before launching an attack.

53. If a prince wants to be a boss in war, he better follow these five principles or he ain't worth squat.

54. If a boss is going up against a big-time enemy, he better keep them from teaming up, and make 'em all scared of him. Then he can take their cities and rule their kingdoms, yo.

This passage emphasizes the importance of preventing the enemy from uniting against you. A successful general must be able to divide and conquer, preventing the enemy from forming a unified front. This can be accomplished through strategic attacks on key targets or through diplomatic maneuvering to create divisions among the enemy.

55. Don't try to be cool with everyone, keep your secrets tight, and then take down your enemies one by one. That's how you win, baby.

A successful general must keep their true intentions hidden and not reveal too much to their allies or enemies. This allows them to maintain an element of surprise and keep their enemies off balance. It's important for a general to be able to strike quickly and decisively, taking advantage of weaknesses in the enemy's defenses.

56. Give out rewards like it's your job, and give orders like there ain't no rules. Then you can run an army like it's one single dude.

A general should be able to adapt quickly and make decisions without being bound by rules or previous arrangements. By doing so, he can motivate his troops and handle the army as though it were a single entity.

This idea of flexibility and adaptability is essential in modern times as well. In today's fast-paced world, a rigid approach can often lead to failure. Instead, leaders must be willing to think outside the box and make unconventional decisions to achieve success.

However, it's important to note that this approach shouldn't be taken to an extreme. Rewards should still be given based on merit and orders should be issued with a clear strategy in mind. As with everything in life, balance is key.

One could say that a general who follows rules like a robot will lead an army of robots. But a general who can think on his feet and adapt to changing circumstances will lead an army of superheroes.

57. Show your squad the plan when it's all good, but keep it quiet when it ain't. And always keep 'em on their toes, ready for whatever comes their way.

A general should never reveal their intentions to their soldiers until the moment of action. By confronting them with the deed itself, the soldiers will be more focused and committed to the task at hand, without having time to doubt or overthink the situation.

This approach can be beneficial in boosting morale and keeping the soldiers on their toes, ready to act quickly and efficiently. By only revealing information when necessary, the general can also avoid creating unnecessary panic or confusion among the troops.

However, it's also important for a leader to find a balance between transparency and secrecy. In some cases, soldiers may benefit from knowing the broader strategic objectives of a campaign, even if they are not privy to all the details.

In a modern context, this principle could be applied to project management or team leadership. Keeping the team focused on the end goal without revealing every detail can help them stay motivated and prevent distractions. However, it's essential to communicate effectively and avoid leaving team members in the dark for too long.

58. If you want your army to survive a deadly situation, just throw them into the fire and watch them rise from the ashes like a phoenix.

When faced with a seemingly impossible situation, soldiers may surprise themselves with their resilience and resourcefulness. Of course, it's important for leaders to carefully weigh the risks before putting their troops in harm's way.

59. When the going gets tough, the tough get going. It's when your army is in dire straits that they find their strength and determination to strike a decisive blow.

This emphasizes the importance of seizing opportunities when they arise. Sometimes it takes a crisis or a setback to motivate soldiers to take bold action and turn the tide of a battle. A skilled leader will be able to recognize these moments and inspire their troops to take advantage of them.

60. To win in war, you need to be as adaptable as a chameleon and adjust your strategy to match your opponent's moves.

 A successful general must be able to anticipate and understand the intentions of their enemy and adjust their strategy accordingly. It's not about blindly charging forward with a predetermined plan, but rather being able to respond to changing circumstances and adapt to the enemy's movements.

 In a modern context, this principle can be applied to many aspects of life, not just warfare. Being adaptable and able to pivot when necessary is a valuable skill in any profession or personal endeavor. The ability to read the situation and adjust one's approach can make the difference between success and failure.

 Personally, I think this principle speaks to the importance of being open-minded and willing to learn from others. It's easy to become entrenched in our own ideas and beliefs, but by taking the time to understand the perspectives and motivations of those around us, we can better navigate any situation and ultimately achieve our goals.

61. If you want to take down the enemy, then constantly harass them from the flanks and pick off their leaders one by one until the head of the snake is gone.

62. The key to success is not just brute force, but also using your wits and cunning to outmaneuver your opponent and achieve your objectives.

In these passage, Sun Tzu emphasizes the importance of persistence and cunning in warfare. By constantly harassing the enemy's flank, a commander can eventually succeed in killing the enemy's commander-in-chief, who is the key to their army's success. This requires patience and the ability to adapt to changing circumstances, as well as the use of tactics such as deception and surprise.

Sun Tzu refers to this ability as "sheer cunning," highlighting the importance of strategic thinking and intelligence gathering in warfare. The ability to outthink and outmaneuver the enemy is just as important as raw strength and firepower.

In modern times, these can still be relevant in both military and non-military contexts. The importance of persistence and adaptability, as well as the use of strategic thinking and cunning, can be applied to many areas of life, from business to personal relationships. It reminds us that success often comes from the ability to think creatively and persistently pursue our goals, even in the face of adversity.

63. When you take command, make a bold statement by cutting off all communication and disrupting the enemy's plans.

This emphasizes the importance of taking immediate action and establishing control as soon as you take command. Sun Tzu suggests cutting off communication and blocking entry points to prevent any potential threats from entering. In modern times, this can be translated to securing digital communication channels and ensuring the security of a company's network. It's a good reminder to be proactive and take necessary precautions when taking charge.

64. Be the boss in the council-chamber and make sure everyone knows who's in charge.

Leaders must assert their authority and maintain control in a council or meeting. It's important to be assertive in order to steer the conversation in the desired direction and prevent any unnecessary debates or disagreements. However, it's important to balance this with being open to others' ideas and opinions. Being too stern can lead to a hostile environment, so it's important to maintain a level of respect and professionalism.

65. When your enemy leaves an opening, don't hesitate to take advantage and strike.

This emphasizes the importance of seizing opportunities when they present themselves in warfare. In battle, the enemy may make a mistake or leave an opening, and it is up to the general to recognize these opportunities and act upon them quickly and decisively.

This principle applies not only to warfare but also to life in general. Opportunities are often fleeting and must be seized upon before they disappear. Waiting for the perfect moment or hesitating can result in missed opportunities and regret.

However, it is also important to exercise caution and not blindly rush in without assessing the situation. Rushing in without a plan or strategy can lead to failure and defeat. As with all of Sun Tzu's teachings, careful planning and strategic thinking are key to success.

Sun Tzu's advice can be applied to many aspects of life beyond warfare, such as business or personal relationships. It is important to keep an eye out for opportunities and be prepared to act quickly when they arise. However, it is equally important to think strategically and not act impulsively without considering the potential risks and consequences.

66. To defeat your enemy, you need to be one step ahead and seize what they hold dear before they even realize it's gone.

Seizing the initiative and take advantage of the enemy's weaknesses. If the opponent holds something dear, such as a strategic location or a valuable resource, the general should aim to capture it before the enemy can reinforce and defend it. Timing is also critical, and the general should aim to arrive on the battlefield when the enemy is least prepared.

In modern warfare, this can be seen in the use of surprise attacks and preemptive strikes. By striking first and seizing key objectives, a military force can gain a significant advantage over the enemy. The use of intelligence and reconnaissance is crucial to identifying the enemy's vulnerabilities and timing the attack.

67. Stick to the rules of warfare and keep adapting until you're in a position to deliver the final blow.

    Play it safe and follow the rules until you see an opening to strike. In other words, bide your time and adapt to the enemy's strategy until you find an advantageous moment to strike.

68. Be patient and bide your time like a coy maiden until your enemy drops their guard, then strike with the speed of a hare and leave them in the dust.

    The idea is to initially appear weak and non-threatening, luring your enemy into a false sense of security, and then strike quickly and decisively.

XII. The Attack by Fire

1. Sun Tzu said: Yo, there are five ways to burn your enemies to a crisp. First, set fire to their camp. Second, burn down their stores. Third, torch their baggage trains. Fourth, light up their arsenals and magazines. And fifth, throw some hot fire bombs right in their face!

2. To pull this off, you gotta have the right tools at the ready. Keep that fire starter kit close, baby!

3. Now, there's a right time and a wrong time to start a fire.

4. Pick a super dry day, and when the moon's in the constellations of the Sieve, the Wall, the Wing, or the Cross-bar. Trust me, those are some windy-ass days.

First off, we've got five ways of attacking with fire. That's a lot of ways! It's like he's saying, "Hey, if you want to win this war, you better bring the heat...literally." The first way is to burn soldiers in their camp, which seems pretty brutal. It's like saying, "Surprise! Your home is on fire, and you're in it." The second way is to burn stores, which is basically the ancient version of looting. The third way is to burn baggage trains, which is like attacking the supply chain. The fourth way is to burn arsenals and magazines, which is basically blowing up the enemy's weapons stash. And the fifth way is to hurl dropping fire amongst the enemy, which sounds like a medieval version of a napalm bomb.

Now, in order to carry out these attacks, we need to have the means available. That means having all the materials for raising fire ready to go. It's like Sun Tzu is saying, "Don't wait until the last minute to start a fire. Get your matches, your lighter fluid, and your kindling all in one place."

But we can't just go around burning stuff willy-nilly. There's a proper season for making attacks with fire, and special days for starting a conflagration. I mean, can you imagine trying to start a fire in the rain? That's like trying to start a party when no one's in the mood. And as for the special days, it's like Sun Tzu is saying, "Hey, let's wait for a windy day and then light everything on fire." It's like the ancient version of waiting for the perfect weather to start a barbecue.

All in all, Sun Tzu's tactics for attacking with fire are pretty intense. But hey, if you're in a war, you gotta do what you gotta do, right? Just make sure you've got your matches ready, and wait for a nice, dry, windy day before you start burning everything in sight.

5. But be warned, when attacking with fire, you gotta be prepared for some possible outcomes.

6. If their camp starts burning from the inside, go ham and attack from the outside.

7. If they're just chillin' while their stuff burns, hold your horses and wait for a better opportunity.

8. When those flames are at their peak, that's your cue to attack if you can.

9. And if you can start the fire from outside their camp, do it at the perfect moment for maximum damage.

These provide guidance on the proper season and special days to launch an attack with fire, as well as five possible developments to be prepared for.

The first development is when fire breaks out inside the enemy's camp, which requires an immediate attack from outside. The second development is when there is an outbreak of fire, but the enemy's soldiers remain quiet, and in this case, one should bide their time and not attack. The third development is when the force of the flames has reached its height, which may present an opportunity for an attack, but if not, one should stay where they are. The fourth development is when it is possible to make an assault with fire from outside, in which case one should not wait for it to break out within, but deliver the attack at a favorable moment. The fifth development is when starting a fire, be sure to be upwind of it and avoid attacking from the downwind.

10. Oh, and one more thing: always attack from upwind. You don't want to be caught in the flames, do you?

11. Just like a good cup of coffee, a strong wind that starts in the morning will keep you going all day, but a gentle night breeze will only give you a temporary boost before you start nodding off.

  Sun Tzu's advice on using fire in warfare is both practical and strategic. He advises waiting for the right season and days with rising winds to increase the effectiveness of the attack. He also provides specific tactics for responding to different scenarios involving fire.

  Sun Tzu also cautions about the direction of the wind when starting a fire. One should always be upwind of the fire to avoid being caught in it. This shows an understanding of how the wind can affect the spread of the fire and the direction it takes. This advice is still relevant today, as we see the devastating effects of wildfires that are often influenced by wind patterns.

Additionally, Sun Tzu's observation about the duration of daytime versus nighttime winds is a reminder of the importance of timing in warfare. Daytime winds tend to last longer, whereas night breezes fade quickly. A strategic general must be aware of the natural patterns and rhythms of the environment to make the most effective decisions.

12. Yo, in any army, you gotta know the five fire developments, calculate star movements, and keep an eye out for the perfect days to strike.

Well, in modern times, we don't necessarily need to rely on the movements of stars to plan our attacks. However, the importance of preparation and understanding the potential outcomes of our actions is still relevant. It's like saying, "know your tools and know your environment before you start a project".

As for the five developments connected with fire, it's still important to be aware of the possible outcomes of our actions, especially in the use of weapons and tactics. So, I would say this quote is still relevant in a more metaphorical sense.

13. Those who use fire to attack are smart, while those who use water to attack get a boost in strength.

Sun Tzu is saying that those who use fire strategically demonstrate intelligence because fire can be a powerful weapon in the right circumstances. On the other hand, those who use water as an aid to the attack gain strength because water can be used to slow down an enemy's advance or create obstacles that they have to navigate around.

14. Water can intercept an enemy, but it can't take all their stuff. Bummer.

Water can be used to intercept an enemy, but not to take everything they have. In other words, you can use water to slow down an enemy's advance or create obstacles that they have to navigate around, but you can't use water to completely defeat them or take everything they have.

In modern terms, we might think of this as saying that while obstacles can slow down an opponent, they can't completely stop them. It's important to remember that even if you're able to create obstacles or setbacks for your opponent, they will still find a way to keep moving forward.

15. If you try to win battles without taking risks and being enterprising, you're in for a world of hurt. It's like trying to run a marathon without training – you're just gonna waste time and be stuck in one spot.

This passage is all about the importance of taking risks and being adventurous in your approach. Sun Tzu believes that if you try to win without taking chances, you'll just end up wasting your time and not making any progress. In modern terms, this could mean that if you always play it safe and never take risks, you won't achieve anything significant in your endeavors. So, don't be afraid to take chances and try new things in order to achieve success.

16. So, as the saying goes: A smart ruler plans ahead, and a good general builds up their resources.

Planning and preparation are crucial in both ruling and warfare. A good leader must anticipate and prepare for possible challenges and opportunities, while a good general must constantly cultivate their resources, including troops, supplies, and intelligence. In today's world, this means that effective leadership requires not only strategic thinking but also adaptability and continuous learning.

17. Don't make moves unless you're gonna get something out of it. Don't use your troops unless you gotta. Don't start a fight unless you're backed into a corner.

Sun Tzu advises against making a move, using troops, or fighting a battle unless there is a clear advantage to be gained. This means being patient and waiting for the right opportunity to present itself, rather than rushing into action without a plan. In modern warfare, this could be interpreted as the need for a well-defined and achievable objective, as well as the importance of gathering intelligence and assessing the risks before taking action.

18. Rulers shouldn't send troops out just 'cause they're cranky, and generals shouldn't fight just 'cause they're mad.

This emphasizes the importance of rational decision-making in warfare. Sun Tzu advises that personal emotions should not influence a ruler's decision to send troops to battle, as it may lead to unnecessary conflict and loss of life. Similarly, a general should not engage in a battle simply because of personal grievances, as it may compromise the success of the mission.

In a modern context, this advice still holds true. Leaders should prioritize the well-being of their citizens and act in the best interest of their nation, rather than acting impulsively based on their personal feelings. The decision to engage in military action should be based on a thorough assessment of the situation and the potential consequences, rather than an emotional response.

19. If it's gonna benefit you, make a move forward. If not, chill where you are.

This piece of advice is simple and straightforward, yet important to keep in mind. It is about being strategic and not making hasty decisions. If you have an advantage, go for it and make a move. If you don't, it's better to wait and evaluate the situation. This can be applied to many areas of life, not just warfare.

20. Anger fades, and frustration turns to happiness.

This piece of advice is about the impermanence of emotions. It reminds us that even the strongest feelings can change over time. Anger can subside and turn into happiness, and vexation can give way to contentment. This can be helpful to remember during difficult times, as it provides hope that things can get better.

21. But once a kingdom's gone, it's gone forever. And, um, yeah, dead people can't come back to life.

This advice is a sobering reminder that there are some things that cannot be undone. Once a kingdom has been destroyed, it can never be restored. Similarly, the dead cannot be brought back to life. This highlights the importance of making wise decisions and taking action to prevent irreversible harm.

22. That's why a smart ruler stays on guard, and a good general is always careful. That's how you keep your country chill and your army strong.

Basically, "better safe than sorry." Being cautious and thoughtful in your actions can help prevent mistakes and keep things running smoothly. It's always better to err on the side of caution rather than rushing into something without considering the consequences.

XIII. The Use of Spies

1. Sun Tzu was like, yo, if you raise a huge army and march them all over the place, it's gonna be super expensive and really suck for everyone involved. You'll be spending a thousand ounces of silver a day and causing chaos all over the damn place. Plus, like, 700,000 families are gonna be majorly inconvenienced.

Sun Tzu basically says "going to war is expensive and not great for the people." It's like buying a new car that you can't really afford and putting it on credit - it may seem great at first, but eventually, you'll have to pay it off, and it'll cost you a lot more in the long run. So, before starting a war, leaders should consider the cost and the impact it will have on the people, including the financial burden, social disruption, and human suffering.

2. You might end up facing your enemy for years, just waiting for that one epic battle that decides everything. So, if you're too cheap to spend a measly hundred ounces of silver on gathering intel about your enemy is straight-up messed up.

Sun Tzu's emphasis on the importance of foreknowledge is also applicable in modern times. In today's world, intelligence gathering and analysis play a critical role in military strategy. Leaders must have a clear understanding of their enemies' capabilities and intentions to make informed decisions about when and how to engage in conflict. He says that remaining ignorant of this information is "the height of inhumanity," and that a leader who acts in such a way is no leader at all. This is a classic example of how important it is to have intelligence gathering and not let your ego get in the way. Sun Tzu is basically saying, "Don't be a cheapskate and ignore the enemy's movements just because you don't want to spend money on spies and reconnaissance." In modern times, we have satellite imagery, cyber espionage, and all kinds of high-tech surveillance methods to keep tabs on our enemies. But the lesson still holds true: don't be cheap, invest in intelligence, and don't let your ego cloud your judgment.

3. Seriously, if you're like that, you're not fit to lead anyone, help your ruler, or win battles. You're just a loser.

Sun Tzu is pretty harsh here, but he's got a point. A leader who doesn't invest in his army's welfare or gather intelligence on the enemy is not fit to lead. In modern times, we see leaders who neglect their troops or ignore the intelligence community, and it always ends badly. So, if you want to be a true leader, take care of your troops and gather all the information you can.

4. That's why the smart leaders and generals know that the key to winning is having insider knowledge. Knowing what your enemy is up to before they make their move is the real game-changer.

Foreknowledge is key, people! Sun Tzu knew it, and so should we. The more information you have, the better prepared you are to make strategic decisions and achieve your goals. In modern times, we have so many ways to gather information, from social media to data analytics, and we should take advantage of all of them. The wise leader knows that foreknowledge is power, and that's how you can achieve things that others think are impossible.

5. Look, you can't just summon a spirit and ask them to spill the beans on the enemy's plans. And forget about trying to figure it out by trial and error, or by doing some fancy math.

6. You gotta get the lowdown from other people, ya dig?

Well, it looks like Sun Tzu is telling us that we can't just rely on talking to ghosts to get the intel we need about our enemy's plans.

That's a bummer, but I guess we'll have to make do with other sources of information.

According to Sun Tzu, the best way to get that info is from other people, specifically spies. And he's got a whole list of different types of spies to choose from, which is pretty impressive.

7. That's where spies come in. There's five types:
- (1) local spies,
- (2) inward spies,
- (3) converted spies,
- (4) doomed spies, and
- (5) surviving spies.

8. When you got all five types of spy working together, nobody can crack your system. That's what I call "divine manipulation of the threads." It's the sovereign's ace in the hole.

In modern times, we might call Sun Tzu's approach "intelligence gathering." His emphasis on the use of spies is still relevant today, as countries and corporations use various methods to gather information about their rivals.

The five classes of spies that Sun Tzu outlines are:

Local spies: These are individuals who have access to information within the enemy's territory, such as local residents or workers.

Inward spies: These are people who have infiltrated the enemy's organization and can report back on their activities and plans.

Converted spies: These are individuals who were originally working for the enemy but have been turned to work for the other side.

Doomed spies: These are spies who are sent to gather information but are expected to be caught and killed in the process. The information they provide is often false or misleading.

Surviving spies: These are individuals who are sent to gather information and are expected to return safely with accurate intelligence.

Sun Tzu believes that when all five types of spies are working together, it creates a "divine manipulation of the threads" where the enemy cannot uncover the system. This is the most precious faculty of the sovereign, as it allows them to make strategic decisions based on accurate and up-to-date intelligence.

In modern times, we still use spies and intelligence gathering to gain an advantage over our enemies, whether it be in military operations or business dealings. However, the methods and technology used have evolved greatly since Sun Tzu's time. Regardless, the concept of having an edge through information is still very relevant today.

9. So you want to get the inside scoop on the enemy, eh? Well, that means cozying up to the locals in their hood.

10. And if you want to really get down and dirty with the enemy's secrets, you gotta use their own officials against them. It's like playing chess with their pawns!

11. Now, if you really want to mess with their minds, you gotta turn their own spies into double agents. It's like Inception, but with spies!

The concept of converted spies is still relevant, as intelligence agencies often try to flip or turn an enemy spy to work for their own side.

12. And for that extra spice of deception, you gotta do some things out in the open that seem fishy, but are actually part of your grand plan. That way, when your spies report back to the enemy, they'll be none the wiser!

The use of doomed spies for deception is also a common tactic, where a government or military may plant false information or signals to mislead their opponents.

13. Don't forget about the surviving spies, though. They're the ones who risk their necks to bring you the enemy's dirty little secrets. Treat 'em well and keep 'em close!

Surviving spies, however, play a critical role in modern intelligence gathering, providing valuable information on the enemy's movements, intentions, and capabilities. The use of technology such as satellite imagery, drone surveillance, and cyber espionage has revolutionized the art of spying, but human intelligence remains an essential component of any successful operation.

While the use of spies can be a necessary and effective tool, it is also a dangerous game. The risk of exposure and retaliation is high, and the consequences can be severe. Therefore, it is crucial to maintain secrecy and ensure that spies are managed with benevolence and straightforwardness, as Sun Tzu advised.

In today's world, where conflicts can be fought not just on the battlefield but also in cyberspace and through covert operations, the lessons of Sun Tzu's teachings on the use of spies are still relevant and valuable.

14. Seriously, don't underestimate the power of a good spy. They're like your best buds, but with top-secret clearance. Shower 'em with rewards and keep your lips sealed tighter than a pickle jar.

So, Sun Tzu says that spies are super important in the army, like, even more important than your bestie or your boo-thang. And you better treat them right too, because they're not gonna risk their lives for peanuts. Plus, you gotta keep their identities on the down-low, or else they might as well be posting their whereabouts on social media.

15. But let's be real, you can't just hire any old Joe Schmoe off the street to be a spy. You gotta have that sixth sense, that gut feeling that tells you when something's not quite right.

16. And once you got your spies on board, don't go messing around with their heads. Be straight up with 'em and treat 'em like you'd wanna be treated. It's like the Golden Rule, but for espionage.

17. Oh, and if you're not quick on your feet and sharp as a tack, you ain't gonna be able to tell the real intel from the fake news. Gotta have that subtle ingenuity, baby.

A leader must be benevolent and straightforward with their spies, treating them with respect and fairness. This will encourage loyalty and trust, which are essential for obtaining reliable information.

At the same time, a leader must also be clever and subtle, using their ingenuity to verify the accuracy of the information provided by their spies. This involves understanding the motives and biases of the spy, as well as the potential for misinformation or deception. By combining benevolence and straightforwardness with subtle ingenuity, a leader can maximize the usefulness of their spies and gain a strategic advantage over their enemies.

In a modern context, these principles can still be applied in fields such as business, politics, and even personal relationships. Building trust and treating others fairly is important for maintaining positive relationships and gathering useful information, while also being vigilant and skeptical about potential biases or hidden agendas.

18. Bottom line: use your spies for everything under the sun. Need to take down an army? Check. Gonna storm a city? Check. Want to take out an individual? Check, check, and check.

Ah, the art of spying! Sun Tzu really knew what he was talking about. To be a successful spy, you need to be subtle, and you need to be ready for any kind of task. Want to find out who your crush is dating? Use your spy skills. Want to know what your boss is planning for the next meeting? Use your spy skills. Want to find out who ate the last slice of pizza in the fridge? Use your spy skills.

19. But hey, if one of your spies spills the beans too soon, you gotta make an example out of 'em. It's like that saying, loose lips sink ships. Except in this case, loose lips get spies killed.

Okay, okay, let's take it down a notch. I don't think we need to be putting spies to death for every little mistake they make. Maybe just take away their spy gadgets for a day or two. But in all seriousness, the importance of secrecy cannot be overstated when it comes to spying. One slip-up could mean the difference between success and failure.

20. You gotta know the enemy like the back of your hand. Get the deets on their attendants, aides-de-camp, door-keepers, and sentries. It's like playing a game of Guess Who, but with real-life consequences.

Sun Tzu is absolutely right on this one. To achieve any goal, you need to know your enemy. And the first step in that process is finding out who their key players are. Whether you're trying to take down an army or just trying to get that promotion at work, you need to know who you're up against. So, go ahead and commission those spies to gather intel on your enemies, but please, no putting them to death if they mess up.

21. Alright folks, listen up. If we catch any enemy spies snooping around, we gotta butter them up, bribe them with some goodies, and give them a nice cozy bed to sleep in. That way, they'll start to feel all warm and fuzzy towards us and might even join our team.

In modern times, this concept of turning enemy spies into converted spies can be seen in the field of intelligence and counterintelligence. Often, intelligence agencies use various tactics, such as blackmail or coercion, to turn enemy spies into double agents who work for their own country's intelligence agency.

22. Once we've got a few converted spies on our side, we can start gathering intel on the enemy with local and inward spies.

Once a spy has been turned, they can provide valuable information about the enemy's network of spies, which can be used to identify and recruit local and inward spies. This can be seen in the practice of counterintelligence, where intelligence agencies work to identify and neutralize enemy spies within their own country.

23. And you know what's even better? We can trick the enemy by feeding them false information through our doomed spy. That'll throw 'em off our scent.

Using the information provided by a converted spy, an intelligence agency can plant false information with a doomed spy who is expected to be caught by the enemy. This can be a tactic to mislead the enemy or to provide disinformation, leading them to make poor strategic decisions.

24. Last but not least, the surviving spy can be put to use when we need them most.

A surviving spy is one who has successfully infiltrated the enemy's camp and returned with valuable information. This information can be used by military strategists to plan their next move. In modern times, surviving spies are often referred to as "assets" and are highly valued by intelligence agencies. In modern times, intelligence agencies rely heavily on human intelligence (HUMINT) gathered by surviving spies or assets. These individuals may be trained agents or recruited from the local population, depending on the circumstances. They may use a variety of tactics to gather information, including covert operations, surveillance, and communication interception. The information they gather can help protect national security and prevent terrorist attacks, among other things.

25. The whole point of this spying business is to get intel on the enemy. And guess what? We can only get that intel from our converted spy. So be nice to 'em and treat 'em like kings and queens.

In modern times, spying may not be as glamorous or mysterious as we see in movies and TV shows, but the principles remain the same. The goal is to gather information on the enemy, and the best source of that information is a converted spy. So if you want to win, you gotta treat your spies right.

26. Fun fact: the rise of the Yin and Chou dynasties was all thanks to some savvy folks who used spying to their advantage. So let's take a page out of their book, shall we?

The rise of many powerful nations was due in part to their ability to gather intelligence, often from spies who had previously served their enemies. It's a time-tested strategy that has worked for centuries.

27. Only the smartest of the smart, the brightest of the bright, will know how to use spies to their fullest potential. Spies are like water to an army, they keep us moving and grooving.

    Spying should never be used for malicious purposes, and the spies themselves must be treated with respect and fairness. The use of spies is like the element of water - it's necessary for an army's ability to move and adapt to its surroundings.

Spying has come a long way since Sun Tzu's time. With advancements in technology, we have drones, satellites, and even spyware that can be installed on electronic devices. But even with all these technological marvels, human intelligence gathering is still a vital component of espionage.

    In today's world, spies are not just used in military operations, but also in business, politics, and even entertainment industries. Imagine a spy infiltrating a rival company to gather intel on their latest product or a politician using a spy to gather dirt on their opponent. And let's not forget about the entertainment industry, where celebrity spies are hired to keep tabs on their rivals' latest projects and personal lives.

    But as Sun Tzu warns, the success of a spy mission depends on the intuitive sagacity of the spy and the subtle ingenuity of the mind managing them. Spies must be treated with utmost benevolence and straightforwardness to ensure their loyalty, and the truth of their reports can only be guaranteed through careful analysis.

Furthermore, as Sun Tzu notes, the converted spy is the most valuable asset in espionage. It is through their information that local and inward spies can be employed, and false information can be spread to the enemy through doomed spies. And finally, the surviving spy, who successfully infiltrates the enemy camp and returns with valuable information, is the ultimate prize.

In conclusion, while spying may have evolved over the centuries, the fundamental principles outlined by Sun Tzu still hold true. Whether you're a military strategist or a business mogul, the ability to gather and analyze intelligence is a vital tool in achieving success. And as Sun Tzu wisely states, only the enlightened ruler and the wise general will use the highest intelligence of their organization for purposes of spying and thereby achieve great results.